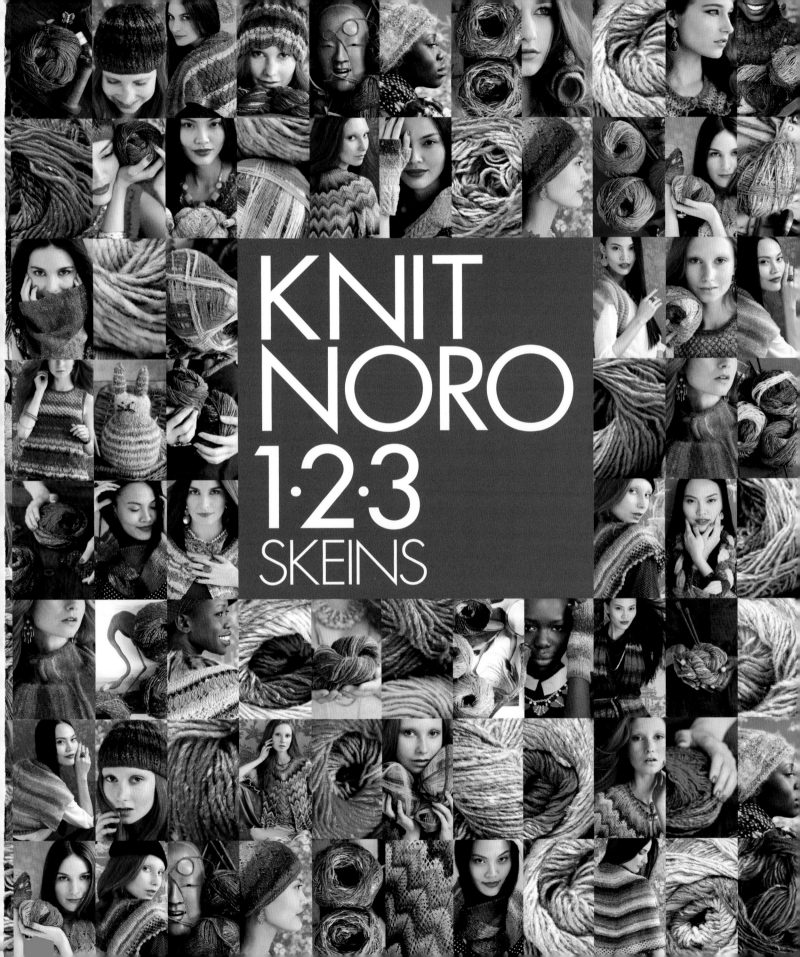

KNIT NORO
1·2·3
SKEINS

KNIT NORO

1·2·3 SKEINS

30 COLORFUL KNITS

sixth&spring books
NEW YORK

Editorial Director **JOY AQUILINO**

Developmental Editor **LISA SILVERMAN**

Yarn Editor **CHRISTINA BEHNKE**

Supervising Patterns Editor **LORI STEINBERG**

Patterns Editors **RACHEL MAURER**

STEPHANIE MRSE

AMY POLCYN

SANDI PROSSER

Proofreader **KRISTIN M. JONES**

Technical Illustrations **LORI STEINBERG**

Photography **ROSE CALLAHAN**

Stylist **KHALIAH JONES**

Hair and Makeup **SOKPHALLA BAN**

Vice President **TRISHA MALCOLM**

Publisher **CARRIE KILMER**

Creative Director **JOE VIOR**

Production Manager **DAVID JOINNIDES**

President **ART JOINNIDES**

Chairman **JAY STEIN**

ISBN: 978-1-936096-69-5

Library of Congress Cataloging-in-Publication Data can be found at
the Library of Congress.

Manufactured in China

1 3 5 7 9 10 8 6 4 2

First Edition

sixth&spring books

161 Avenue of the Americas • New York, New York 10013

sixthandspringbooks.com

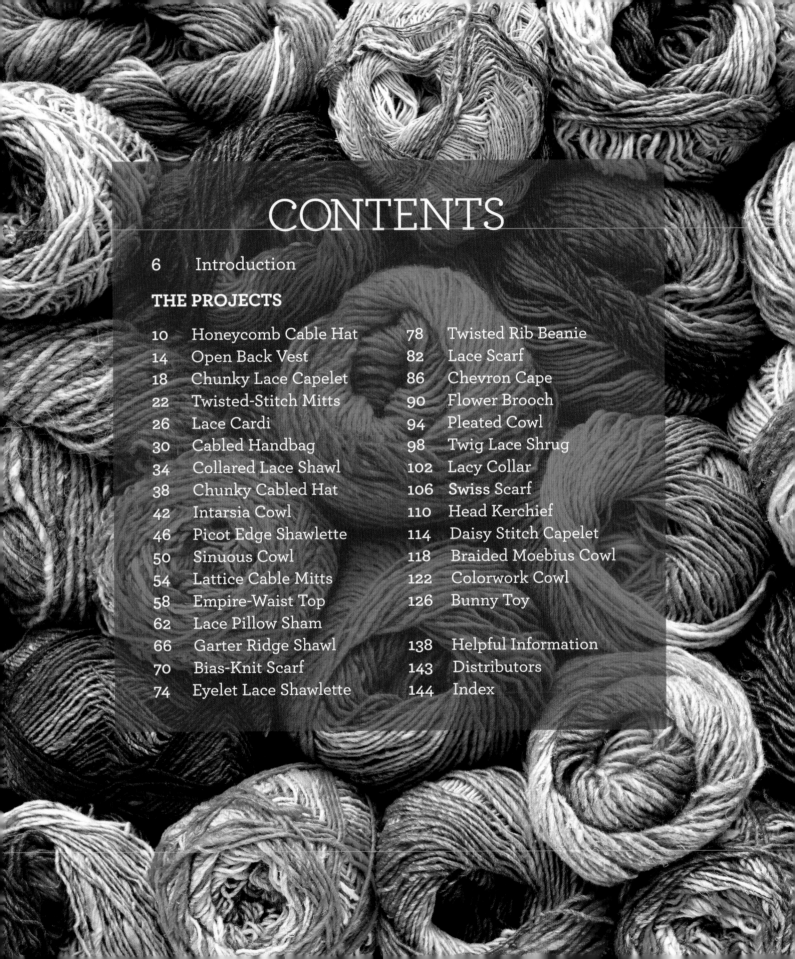

CONTENTS

INTRODUCTION

The first three books in the Knit Noro series, *Knit Noro*, *Knit Noro Accessories*, and *Crochet Noro*, all demonstrated the versatility of Noro yarns with a breathtaking array of projects by some of the top designers in knitting and crochet. Now, in *Knit Noro 1 2 3 Skeins*, a whole new world of possibilities is revealed—the world of knits that can be created with only a few skeins of yarn. From exquisite accessories to beautifully imagined garments, the projects in this book prove that a "small" project can feel anything but small.

Eisaku Noro has been creating his world-renowned yarns in Japan's Aichi province for more than forty years. Spun from the finest natural materials with great respect for environmental concerns, these spectacular yarns are dyed exclusively by hand into a dazzling array of colors. The patterns in this artful collection employ several popular Noro yarns, including Silk Garden, Silk Garden Lite, Kureyon, Taiyo, and Taiyo Sock, along with newer favorites such as Kirara and Obi.

In the hands of the right designers, even a small amount of Noro yarn can be manipulated in ways that show off its breathtaking colorways and unique natural textures to their best effect. From intricate lace to chunky cables to stripes formed from different sections of the same skein, you'll find a full range of knitting techniques in this book, resulting in a spectacular array of designs that will be a joy to knit, whether you're a longtime Noro lover or a Noro newbie.

With patterns suited for every style and skill level, stunning full-color photography, and clearly laid-out instructions, *Knit Noro 1 2 3 Skeins* is not only full of knitted works of art; it's a work of art in itself—just like every skein of Noro.

The Projects

Two Skeins

Honeycomb Cable Hat

Honeycomb Cable Hat

The eye-catching scalloped brim of this hat can also be cuffed for a less slouchy look.

Designed by Jacqueline Van Dillen

Skill Level:

■■■□

Materials

■ 2 1³⁄₄oz/50g skeins (each approx 164yd/150m) of Noro *Kirara* (wool/cotton/silk/angora) in #13 wine/orange/purple/hot pink (④)
■ One pair size 4 (3.5mm) needles OR SIZE TO OBTAIN GAUGE
■ Cable needle (cn)
■ Stitch markers

Size

Instructions are written for one size.

Knitted Measurements

Circumference at brim, slightly stretched 22"/56cm
Length (including brim) 11"/28cm

Gauge

26 sts and 30 rows to 4"/10cm over cable pat using size 4 (3.5mm) needles. TAKE TIME TO CHECK GAUGE.

Stitch Glossary

4-st RC Sl 2 sts to cn and hold to *back*, k2, k2 from cn.
3-st RC Sl 1 st to cn and hold to *back*, k2, k1 from cn.
3-st LC Sl 2 sts to cn and hold to *front*, k1, k2 from cn.

Notes

1) Hat is worked flat and seamed up the back.
2) Charts can be found on page 130.

Hat

Cast on 142 sts.
Beg chart 1
Row 1 (RS) Work to rep line, work 14-st rep 9 times across, work to end of chart.
Cont to work chart in this manner until row 44 is complete, rep rows 1–34 once more.
Beg chart 2
Next row (RS) Work to rep line, work 14-st rep 9 times, work to end of chart.
Cont to work chart in this manner until row 10 is complete—62 sts.
Crown shaping
Next row (RS) K1, *k2tog; rep from * to last st, k1—32 sts.
Next row Purl.
Next row (RS) *K2tog; rep from * to end of row—16 sts.
Next row Purl.
Next row (RS) *K2tog; rep from * to end of row—8 sts.
Break yarn, leaving a 20"/50cm tail. Thread tail through rem sts and fasten off. Sew center back seam, reversing seam for last 1¹⁄₄"/3cm for brim turn-back. ❖

Two Skeins

Open Back Vest

14

Open Back Vest

I-cord ties st the waist turn a simple ribbed and cabled rectangle into a chic year-round layer.

Designed by Jacqueline Van Dillen

Skill Level:

■■□□

Materials

- 2 3½oz/100g skeins (each approx 220yd/200m) of Noro *Taiyo* (cotton/silk/wool/nylon) in #41 red/olive/black/purple (4)
- One pair size 8 (5mm) needles OR SIZE TO OBTAIN GAUGE
- One set (2) size 8 (5mm) double-pointed needles (dpns)
- Cable needle (cn)
- 1 snap, ¾" diameter
- Removable stitch markers

Sizes

Instructions are written for size Small. Changes for Medium and Large are in parentheses.

Knitted Measurements

Length from lower edge to center back neck approx 27¼ (29¼, 31¼)"/69 (74.5, 80)cm
Front width (slightly stretched) 22½"/57cm

Gauge

14 sts and 22 rows to 4"/10cm over rib pat using size 8 (5mm) needles. TAKE TIME TO CHECK GAUGE.

Stitch Glossary

6-st RC Sl 3 sts to cn and hold to *back*, k3, k3 from cn.

Rib Pattern

(multiple of 8 sts)
Row 1 (RS) P2, *k4, p4; rep from * to last 6 sts, k4, p2.
Row 2 K2, *p4, k4; rep from * to last 6 sts, p4, k2.
Rep rows 1 and 2 for rib pat.

Cable Pattern

(worked over 6 sts)
Rows 1 and all WS rows P6.
Rows 2, 4, 8, and 10 K6.
Row 6 6-st RC.
Rep rows 1–10 for cable pat.

Note

Vest is worked in one piece, starting at lower right front edge and ending at lower left front edge.

Vest

With straight needles, cast on 40 sts. Work in rib pat until piece measures 10"/25.5cm, end with a WS row. Place marker (pm) at each end of last row worked for armhole.
Right armhole shaping
Next row (RS) Work in pat to last 4 sts, k2tog, p2—39 sts.
Next row Work even in pat.
Rep last 2 rows 7 times more—32 sts.
Beg cable pat
Next (inc) row (RS) P2, k4, [p4, k1, M1, k2, M1, k1] twice, p4, k4, p2—36 sts.
Next row (WS) Work 10 sts in pat, work row 1 of cable pat over next 6 sts, p4, work row 1 of cable pat over next 6 sts, work in pat to end of row.
Cont in this manner, working appropriate row of cable pat, until

piece measures approx 34½ (38½, 42½)"/87.5 (98, 108)cm from armhole markers, end with a row 1 of cable pat.

Next (dec) row (RS) P2, k4, [p4, k2tog, k2, k2tog] twice, work in pat to end of row—32 sts.

Next row K2, *p4, k4; rep from * to last 6 sts, p4, k2.

Left armhole shaping

Next row (RS) Work in pat to last 2 sts, M1, p2—33 sts.

Next row Work even in pat.

Rep last 2 rows 7 times more—40 sts.

Pm for left armhole at each end of last row.

Work even in rib pat until piece measures 10"/25.5cm from left armhole marker, end with a WS row. Bind off in pat.

Finishing
I-cord back ties (make 2)

With dpns, cast on 6 sts. *Knit one row. Without turning work, slide sts to opposite end of row. Pull yarn tightly from end of row. Rep from * until I-cord measures approx 31½"/80cm or desired length. Bind off knitwise.

Sew cast-on end of each I-cord to armhole edge at armhole markers.

Sew snap fastener to center fronts at markers, lapping left front over right front. ♣

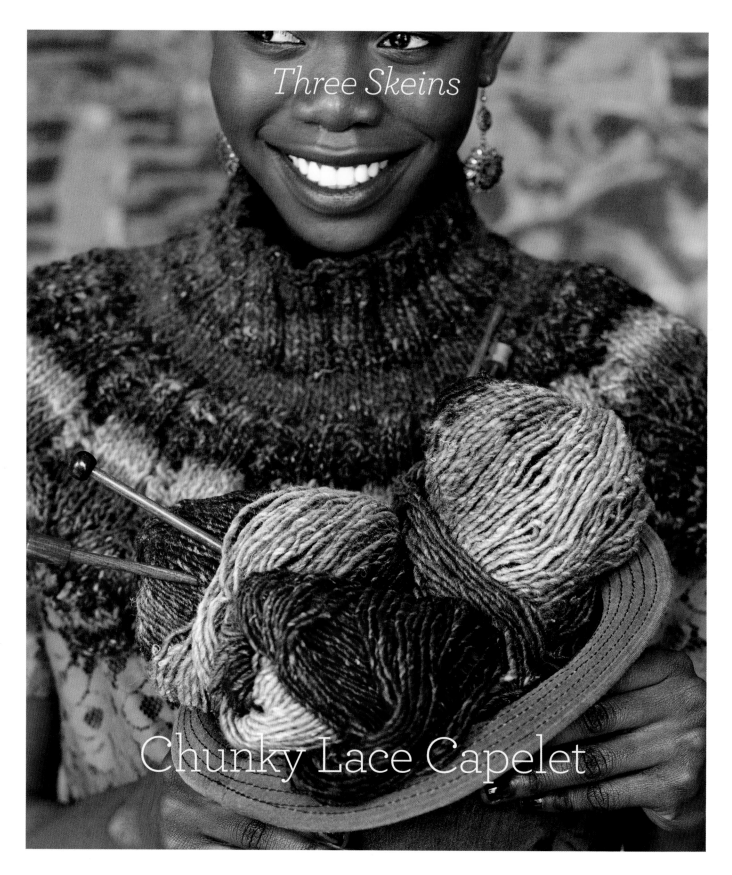

Three Skeins

Chunky Lace Capelet

Chunky Lace Capelet

Keep warm with flair in this capelet with a cozy turtleneck, eyelet details, and a scalloped edge.

Designed by Carol Sulcoski

Skill Level:

■■■□

Materials
- 3 1¾oz/50g skeins (each approx 82yd/75m) of Noro *Kama* (wool/silk/alpaca/kid mohair/angora) in #31 purple/lilac/green 🔵
- One each sizes 9 and 10½ (5.5 and 6.5mm) circular needle, 24"/60cm long, OR SIZE TO OBTAIN GAUGE
- Stitch marker

Size
Instructions are written for one size.

Knitted Measurements
Circumference at hem 40"/101.5cm
Circumference at top edge (slightly stretched) 20"/51cm
Length approx 10½"/26.5cm

Gauge
16 sts and 24 rnds to 4"/10cm over St st using size 9 (5.5mm) needles. TAKE TIME TO CHECK GAUGE.

Stitch Glossary
MB (make bobble) K1 in the front, back, and front of next st; turn, p3, turn, SK2P.

Edging Pattern
(multiple of 10 sts)
Rnd 1 *Yo, k3, SK2P, k3, yo, k1; rep from * to end.
Rnd 2 Knit.
Rnd 3 *K1, yo, k2, sk2p, k2, yo, k1, p1; rep from * to end.
Rnd 4 *K9, p1; rep from * to end.
Rnd 5 *K2, yo, k1, SK2P, k1, yo, k2, p1; rep from * to end.
Rnd 6 *K9, p1; rep from * to end.
Rnd 7 *K3, yo, SK2P, yo, k3, p1; rep from * to end.
Rnd 8 Knit.
Rep rnds 1–8 for edging pat.

Note
Capelet is knit in the round from bottom edge to collar.

Capelet
With larger needle, cast on 180 sts. Join and place marker (pm) for beg of rnd, being careful not to twist sts.
Set-up rnd *P4, MB, p5; rep from * to end.
Beg with rnd 1, work 10-st rep of edging pat 18 times around.
Cont to work edging pat in this manner until rnd 8 is complete.
Rep rnds 1–8 once more.
Rnd 17 *K3, yo, SK2P, yo, k4; rep from * to end.
Rnd 18 Knit.
Change to smaller needle.
Rnd 19 (dec) *K1, ssk, yo, SK2P, yo, k2tog, k2; rep from * to end—144 sts.
Rnds 20, 22, and 24 Knit.
Rnds 21 and 23 *K2, yo, SK2P, yo, k3; rep from * to end.
Rnd 25 (dec) *Ssk, yo, SK2P, yo, k2tog, k1; rep from * to end—108 sts.
Rnds 26, 28, and 30 Knit.
Rnds 27 and 29 *K1, yo, SK2P, yo, k2; rep from * to end.
Rnd 31 (dec) *K1, yo, SK2P, yo, k2tog; rep from * to end—90 sts.
Rnd 32 Knit.
Rnd 33 *K1, yo, SK2P, yo, k1; rep from * to end.
Knit 9 rnds.
Next rnd *K3, p2; rep from * to end.
Rep last rnd for 3"/7.5cm. Bind off in rib. ✿

One Skein

Twisted-Stitch Mitts

Twisted-Stitch Mitts

A muted palette of greens and browns brings texture to the forefront and evokes the transition from autumn to winter.

Designed by Tammy Eigeman Thompson

Skill Level:
■■■□

Materials
- 1 3½oz/100g skein (each approx 462yd/422m) of Noro *Taiyo Sock* (cotton/wool/nylon/silk) in #39 greens/neutrals ❶
- One set (5) each sizes 1 and 2 (2.25 and 2.75mm) double-pointed needles (dpns), OR SIZE TO OBTAIN GAUGE
- Cable needle (cn)
- Stitch markers
- Scrap yarn

Size
Instructions are written for one size.

Knitted Measurements
Hand circumference 8"/20.5cm
Length 7¼"/18.5cm

Gauge
38 sts and 36 rows to 4"/10cm over cable pat (chart 2) using size 2 (2.75mm) needles. TAKE TIME TO CHECK GAUGE.

Stitch Glossary
2-st RC Sl 1 st to cn and hold to *back*, k1, k1 from cn.
2-st LPC Sl 1 st to cn and hold to *front*, p1, k1 from cn.
2-st RPC Sl 1 st to cn and hold to *back*, k1, p1 from cn.
3-st LC Sl 2 sts to cn and hold to *front*, k1, k2 from cn.
4-st LC Sl 2 sts to cn and hold to *front*, k2, k2 from cn.
4-st RC Sl 2 sts to cn and hold to *back*, k2, k2 from cn.
4-st RPC Sl 2 sts to cn and hold to *back*, k2, p2 from cn.
4-st LPC Sl 2 sts to cn and hold to *front*, p2, k2 from cn.

Note
Charts can be found on page 131.

Left Mitt
Cuff
With larger needles, cast on 72 sts. Pm for beg of rnd and join, being careful not to twist sts. Knit 1 rnd.
Begin chart 1
Rnd 1 Work 24-st chart rep 3 times around.
Cont to work chart in this way until rnd 6 is complete. Rep rnds 1–6 for 3 times more.
Knit 1 rnd. Change to smaller needles. Knit 1 rnd.
Next (dec) rnd *K1, k2tog; rep from * around—48 sts.
Work in k1, p1 rib for 7 rnds.
Next (inc) rnd *K8, M1; rep from * around—54 sts.
Begin chart 2
Next rnd Work chart 2 over 27 sts (back of hand), pm, work in k1, p1 rib over rem 27 sts (palm).
Cont to work in this way until rnd 4 of chart 2 is complete.
Thumb gusset
Next rnd Work rnd 5 of chart 2, sl marker, rib to last st, pm, k1 (thumb gusset).
Next (inc) rnd Work to 2nd marker, sl marker, M1, k1, M1—2 sts inc.
Next rnd Work to 2nd marker, work gusset sts in rib pat.
Next (inc) rnd Work in pat to 2nd marker, sl marker, M1, work in rib to end, M1—2 sts inc.

Rep last 2 rnds until there are 15 gusset sts between markers. Slip gusset sts to scrap yarn for thumb. Cast on 1 st over gap—54 sts. Cont in pats, working chart 2 on back of hand and rib pat on palm until rnd 30 of chart 2 is complete. Change to smaller needles.
Next rnd K27, work in rib to end of rnd.
Work 3 rnds in k1, p1 rib over all sts. Bind off.
Thumb
Place 15 thumb sts on larger dpns. Pick up and k 5 sts along thumb opening—20 sts. Work in k1, p1 rib for 5 rnds. Bind off.

Right Mitt
Cuff
Work as for left mitt until rnd 4 of chart 2 is complete.
Thumb gusset
Next rnd Work rnd 5 of chart 2, sl marker, k1 (thumb gusset), pm, work in rib to end of rnd.
Next (inc) rnd Work to first marker, sl marker, M1, k1, M1, sl marker, work to end—2 sts inc.
Next rnd Work to first marker, work gusset sts in rib pat, work to end of rnd.
Next (inc) rnd Work to first marker, sl marker, M1, rib to next marker, M1, work to end of rnd—2 sts inc.
Complete as for left mitt. ❧

Two to Three Skeins

Lace Cardi

Lace Cardi

A chevron lace pattern worked in a bright and luminous colorway makes this airy jacket a showstopper.

Designed by Brooke Nico

Skill Level:
■■■■

Materials
- 2 (3) 3½oz/100g skeins (each approx 920yd/841m) of Noro *Taiyo Lace* (cotton/silk/wool/nylon) in #1 yellows/greens/purples (◐0)
- One each size 2 (2.75mm) circular needles, 24"/61cm and 40"/101cm long, OR SIZE TO OBTAIN GAUGE
- One set (5) size 2 (2.75mm) double-pointed needles (dpns)
- One pair size 1 (2.25mm) needles
- Size E/4 (3.5mm) crochet hook
- Stitch holders
- Stitch markers
- One 1"/25mm button

Sizes
Instructions are written for size X-Small/Small. Changes for Medium/Large are in parentheses. (Shown in size X-Small/Small.)

Knitted Measurements
Bust (closed) 34½ (42)"/87.5 (106.5)cm
Length 21 (23)"/53.5 (58.5)cm
Upper arm 9½ (11)"/24 (28)cm

Gauge
36 sts and 28 rows to 4"/10cm over lace pat using size 2 (2.75mm) needles (after blocking). TAKE TIME TO CHECK GAUGE.

Gauge Swatch
With shorter circular needle, cast on 36 sts. Work in lace pat as foll:
Row 1 (RS) K3, *k2tog, yo, k1, yo, ssk; rep from *, end k3.
Row 2 Purl. Rep these 2 rows 13 times more. Bind off loosely knitwise. Piece should measure 4 x 4"/10 x 10cm after blocking.

Notes
1) Jacket is worked from the neckband down to bottom edge of peplum.
2) Circular needle is used to accommodate large number of sts. Do not join.
3) Chart 1, for peplum, shows RS rows only; purl all WS rows.
4) Chart 2, for cuff, shows odd rounds only; knit all even rounds.
5) Charts can be found on page 132.

Stitch Glossary
ch Crochet chain st.
sc Single crochet.

Cardigan
Yoke
With straight needles, cast on 76 (82) sts.
Row 1 (RS) K3, *p1, k2; rep from *, end k1.
Row 2 P3, *k1, p2; rep from *, end p1.
Rep rows 1 and 2 twice more.
For size Medium/Large only
Rep row 1 once more.
Next row P3, *M1 p-st, p7; rep from *, end M1 p-st, p2—94 sts.
For both sizes
Change to shorter circular needle. Cont on 76 (94) sts as foll:
Beg lace pat
Row (inc) 1 (RS) K3, *yo, k1, yo, k2; rep from *, end k1—124 (154) sts.
Row 2 Purl.
Row 3 K2, *k2tog, yo, k1, yo, ssk; rep from *, end k2.
Row 4 Purl.
Rep rows 3 and 4 until piece measures 2"/5cm from beg (slightly stretched), end with a row 4.
Row (inc) 5 (RS) K3, *[yo, k1] 3 times, yo, k2; rep from *, end k1—220 (274) sts.

Row 6 Purl.

Row (inc) 7 K2, *k2tog, [k1, yo] 4 times, k1, ssk; rep from *, end k2—268 (334) sts.

Row 8 Purl.

Row 9 K2, *[k2tog] twice, [yo, k1] 3 times, yo, [ssk] twice; rep from *, end k2.

Row 10 Purl.

Rep rows 9 and 10 until piece measures 6"/15cm from beg (slightly stretched), end with row 10.

Row (inc) 11 (RS) K2, *k2tog, k1, [yo, k1] 6 times, ssk; rep from *, end k2—364 (454) sts.

Row 12 Purl.

Row (inc) 13 K2, *[k2tog] twice, k1, [yo, k1] 6 times, [ssk] twice; rep from *, end k2—412 (514) sts.

Row 14 Purl.

Row 15 K2, *[k2tog] 3 times, [yo, k1] 5 times, yo, [ssk] 3 times; rep from *, end k2.

Row 16 Purl.

Rep rows 15 and 16 until piece measures 9 (10)"/23 (25.5)cm from beg (slightly stretched), end with row 15 (RS).

Separate for body and sleeves

Next row (WS) P70 (87) for left front, place next 68 (85) sts on holder for left sleeve, cast on 17 sts for left underarm, p136 (170) for back, place next 68 (85) sts on holder for right sleeve, cast on 17 sts for right underarm, p70 (87) for right front—310 (378) sts.

Rep rows 15 and 16 twice more. Cont in lace pat as foll:

Row (inc) 17 (RS) K2, *[k2tog] twice, k1, [yo, k1] 8 times, [ssk] twice; rep from *, end k2—382 (466) sts.

Row 18 Purl.

Row (inc) 19 K2, *[k2tog] 3 times, k1, (yo, k1) 8 times, [ssk] 3 times; rep from *, end k2—418 (510) sts.

Row 20 Purl.

Row 21 K2, *[k2tog] 4 times, [yo, k1] 7 times, yo, [ssk] 4 times; rep from *, end k2.

Row 22 Purl.

Rep rows 21 and 22 until piece measures 5 (6)"/12.5 (15)cm from underarm, end with row 22.

Row (inc) 23 K2, *[k2tog] 3 times, k1, [yo, k1] 10 times, [ssk] 3 times; rep from *, end k2—490 (598) sts.

Row 24 Purl.

Row (inc) 25 K2, *[k2tog] 4 times, k1, [yo, k1] 10 times, [ssk] 4 times; rep from *, end k2—526 (642) sts.

Row 26 Purl.

Row 27 K2, *[k2tog] 5 times, [yo, k1] 9 times, yo, [ssk] 5 times; rep from *, end k2.

Row 28 Purl.

Rep rows 27 and 28 seven times more.

Beg chart 1 (peplum)

Row 1 (RS) K2, place marker (pm), work to rep line, work sts

between rep lines 17 (21) times, pm, k2.

Row 2 P2, sl marker, purl to next marker, sl marker, p2. Keeping 2 sts each side in St st, cont to foll chart in this manner through row 35. Bind off all sts loosely purlwise.

Sleeves

With RS facing, place 68 (85) sts of first sleeve evenly divided over 4 dpns. Join yarn.

Next rnd K68 (85), cast on 17 sts for underarm—85 (102) sts. Join and pm for beg of rnd. Cont in lace pat as foll:

Rnd 1 *[K2tog] 3 times, [yo, k1] 5 times, yo, [ssk] 3 times; rep from * around.

Rnd 2 Knit.

Rep rnds 1 and 2 for 6 (10) times more.

Beg chart 2 (cuff)

Rnd 1 Work chart 5 (6) times around.

Rnd 2 Knit. Cont to foll chart in this manner through rnd 31. Change to shorter circular needle when needed to accommodate number of sts. Bind off all sts loosely knitwise.

Finishing

Sew underarm seams. Block to measurements.

Left front edging

With RS facing and crochet hook, join yarn with a sl st in top front edge.

Row 1 (RS) Ch 1, making sure that work lies flat, sc evenly to bottom edge. Fasten off.

Right front edging and button loop

With RS facing and crochet hook, join yarn with a sl st in bottom front edge.

Row 1 (RS) Ch 1, making sure that work lies flat, sc evenly to top edge, ch 5 for button loop; turn.

Skip first 4 sc of edging, join with a sl st in next sc; turn. Work 5 sc over ch-5. Join with a sl st in beg ch-1. Fasten off. Sew on button. ♣

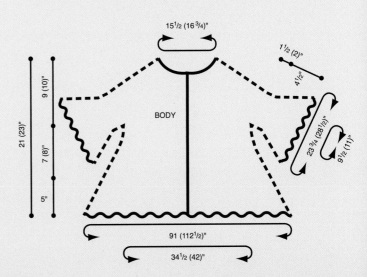

Two Skeins

Cabled Handbag

Cabled Handbag

Bulky yarn and a fabric lining provide structure, while centered cables and a vivid colorway add pizzazz.

Designed by Cheri Esper

Skill Level:
■■■□

Materials
- 2 1¾oz/50g skeins (each approx 98yd/90m) of Noro *Mossa* (wool/rayon/kid mohair/silk/nylon) in #11 charcoal/green/wine/taupe ⑤
- Size 9 (5.5mm) circular needle, 16"/40cm long, OR SIZE TO OBTAIN GAUGE
- Cable needle (cn)
- Stitch markers
- Two circular purse handles, 4½"/11.5cm diameter
- ¼yd/.25m of lining fabric
- Sewing needle and thread to match yarn

Knitted Measurements
Width 10½"/26.5cm
Height 8½"/21.5cm

Gauge
13 sts and 18 rnds to 4"/10cm over St st using size 9 (5.5mm) needles. TAKE TIME TO CHECK GAUGE.

Stitch Glossary
6-st LC Sl 3 sts to cn and hold to *front*, k3; k3 from cn.
6-st RC Sl 3 sts to cn and hold to *back*, k3; k3 from cn.
4-st LPC Sl 3 sts to cn and hold to *front*, p1; k3 from cn.
4-st RPC Sl 1 st to cn and hold to *back*, k3; p1 from cn.

Note
Chart can be found on page 133.

Handbag
Cast on 78 sts. Place marker (pm) for beg of rnd and join, being careful not to twist sts.
Rnd 1 P27, pm, work rnd 1 of chart over next 24 sts, pm, purl to end of rnd.
Rnd 2 P27, sl marker, work rnd 2 of chart over next 24 sts, sl marker, purl to end of rnd.
Cont to work in this way until rnd 28 of chart is complete, then rep rnds 5–24 once more. Bind off in pat.

Finishing
With cable panel at center front, sew cast-on edge together for bottom of bag.
Lining
Trace bag on lining fabric, adding ½"/1.5cm all around. Cut out 2 pieces. With RS facing and using a ½"/1.5cm seam allowance, sew pieces together along side and bottom edges. Turn top edge ½"/1.5cm to WS and press. Insert lining and stitch top edge of lining in place approx ¼"/.5cm below top edge of bag.
Handles
With yarn, sew handles to upper edge of bag at center, with close but not overlapping whipstitches, working around handle and into the bound-off sts at upper edge of bag. ❖

One Skein

Collared Lace Shawl

Collared Lace Shawl

This shawl plays subtly and beautifully with shapes, as the points of the triangle and charming mini-collar echo the allover diamond lace pattern.

Designed by Marin J. Melchior

Skill Level:
■■■□

Materials

■ 1 3½oz/100g skein (each approx 920yd/841m) of Noro *Taiyo Lace* (cotton/silk/wool/nylon) in #5 brown/grey/orange/green **(0)**
■ Size 3 (3.25mm) circular needle, 24"/60cm long, OR SIZE TO OBTAIN GAUGE
■ Stitch markers

Knitted Measurements

Length from back of neck to tip, after blocking 30"/76cm
Width after blocking 45"/114cm

Gauge

28 sts to 5"/12.5cm and 40 rows to 4"/10cm over chart pat using size 3 (3.25mm) needles. TAKE TIME TO CHECK GAUGE.

Short Row Wrap & Turn (w&t)

On RS row (on WS row)
1) Wyib (wyif), sl next st purlwise.
2) Move yarn between the needles to the front (back).
3) Sl the same st back to LH needle. Turn work. One st is wrapped.
4) When working the wrapped st, insert RH needle under the wrap and work it tog with the corresponding st on needle to close the wrap.

Stitch Glossary

S2KP (center double dec) Sl 2 sts tog knitwise, k1, pass sl sts over the k1.

Notes

1) Shawl is worked back and forth in rows. Circular needle is used to accommodate large number of sts. Do not join.
2) Chart can be found on page 134.

Shawl

Cast on 36 sts.
Row 1 (WS) [K1, p1] 9 times, place marker (pm), [p1, k1] 9 times.
Row 2 (RS) Sl 1, work in rib as established to 2 sts before marker; k2tog, sl marker, ssk, work in rib as established to end.
Row 3 Sl 1, work in rib to 2 sts before marker; p2tog tbl, sl marker, p2tog, work in rib to end.
Rep rows 2 and 3 five times more—12 sts. Break yarn, leaving a 6"/15cm tail.
Next row (RS) Rejoin yarn to pick up and k 8 sts along right edge, work 12 sts on needle in pat, pick up and k 8 sts along left edge—28 sts.
Next row Work in rib to marker; remove marker, work in rib to end.
Begin chart
Row 1 (RS) Sl 1, M1, work 5 sts in rib, k2tog, pm, work 5 sts in rib, pm, k1, pm for chart, work chart row, pm for chart, k1, pm, work 5 sts in rib, pm, ssk, work 5 sts in rib, M1, k1—29 sts.
Row 2 (WS) Sl 1, k the knit sts and p the purl sts, working row 2 of chart between chart markers and slipping all markers.
Row 3 Sl 1, M1, work in rib to 2 sts before marker, k2tog, sl marker, work in rib to next marker, sl marker, k1, sl marker, work row 3 of chart, sl marker, k1, sl marker, work in rib to next marker, ssk, work in rib to last st, M1, k1.
Row 4 Work even, incorporating new sts into rib pat and working row 4 of chart between chart markers.

Cont to work in this manner until row 36 of chart is complete. Rep rows 21–36 eleven times more—297 sts.

Upper edge

Row 1 (RS) Sl 1, work in rib to 2 sts before next marker, k2tog, sl marker, M1, work in rib to next marker, remove marker, k1, sl marker, work in rib to next marker, sl marker, k1, remove marker, work in rib to next marker, M1, sl marker, ssk, work in rib to last st, k1.

Row 2 Work even, incorporating new sts into rib pat.

Row 3 Sl 1, work in rib to 2 sts before next marker, k2tog, sl marker, M1, work in rib to 1 st before next marker, k1, sl marker, work in rib to next marker, sl marker, k1, work in rib to next marker, M1, sl marker, ssk, work in rib to last st, k1.

Row 4 Rep row 2.

Row 5 Work as for row 3, working an M1 on either side of center st—2 sts inc.

Rows 6 and 7 Rep rows 4 and 5.

Row 8 Rep row 4.

Row 9 Work to center st, M1, k1, M1, work 5 sts, w&t.

Row 10 Work to 1 st past center st, work 5 sts, w&t.

Rows 11 and 13 Work to center st, M1, k1, M1, work 5 sts after wrapped st (closing wrap), w&t.

Rows 12 and 14 Work to 5 sts after wrapped st (closing wrap), w&t.

Rows 15 and 16 Work in pat to 10 sts after wrapped st, w&t.

Work in rib for 6 rows.

Work in St st (k on RS, p on WS) for 6 rows. Bind off. ♣

One Skein

Chunky Cabled Hat

Chunky Cabled Hat

Feel both warm and whimsical in this plush angora-blend hat topped with fun corkscrew tassels.

Designed by Christy Kay Morse

Skill Level:
■■■□

Materials
- 1 3½oz/100g skein (each approx 142yd/130m) of Noro *Nadeshiko* (angora/wool/silk) in #23 purple/green/blue (5)
- Size 10 (6mm) circular needle, 16"/40.5cm long, OR SIZE TO OBTAIN GAUGE
- One set (5) size 10 (6mm) double-pointed needles (dpns)
- Size J/10 (6mm) crochet hook
- Scrap yarn
- Two cable needles (cn)
- Stitch markers

Size
Instructions are written for one size.

Knitted Measurements
Circumference 20"/50.5cm
Length (not including tassels) approx 7½"/19cm

Gauge
19 sts and 20 rows to 4"/10cm over bridge cable pat using size 10 (6mm) needles. TAKE TIME TO CHECK GAUGE.

Stitch Glossary
9-st RLC Sl 3 sts to cn and hold to *back*, sl next 3 sts to 2nd cn and hold to *front*, k3, k3 from 2nd cn, k3 from first cn.
6-st RC Sl 3 sts to cn and hold to *back*, k3, k3 from cn.
6-st LC Sl 3 sts to cn and hold to *front*, k3, k3 from cn.

Provisional Cast-on
With scrap yarn and crochet hook, ch the number of sts to cast on plus a few extra. Cut a tail and pull the tail through the last chain. With knitting needle and yarn, pick up and knit the stated number of sts through the "purl bumps" on the back of the chain. To remove scrap yarn chain, when instructed, pull out the tail from the last crochet stitch. Gently and slowly pull on the tail to unravel the crochet stitches, carefully placing each released knit stitch on a needle.

Bridge Cable Pattern
Row 1 (RS) P3, k9, p3.
Row 2 K3, p9, k3.
Rows 3–8 Rep rows 1 and 2.
Row 9 P3, 9-st RLC, p3.
Row 10–16 Rep rows 1 and 2, beg with row 2.
Rep rows 1–16 for bridge cable pat.

Hat
Cable band
Cast on 15 sts using provisional cast-on method. Work rows 1–16 of bridge cable pat 6 times. Remove scrap yarn, and place sts on a needle. Graft ends of band tog using Kitchener st.
Crown
With circular needle and RS facing, pick up and k 72 sts around edge of cable band. Place marker (pm) for beg of rnd.
Purl 2 rnds.
Rnds 1 and 2 K1, p2, *k6, p2, k2, p2; rep from * to last 9 sts, k6, p2, k1.
Rnd 3 K1, p2, *6-st RC, p2, k2, p2; rep from * to last 9 sts, 6-st RC, p2, k1.
Rnds 4–8 Rep rnd 1.

Rnd 9 K1, p2, *6-st LC, p2, k2, p2; rep from * to last 9 sts, 6-st LC, p2, k1.

Rnds 10–14 Rep rnd 1.

Rnd 15 (dec) K1, p2tog, *6-st RC, p2tog, k2, p2tog; rep from * to last 9 sts, 6-st RC, p2tog, k1—60 sts.

Rnd 16 K1, p1, *k6, p1, k2, p1; rep from * to last 8 sts, k6, p1, k1.

Rnd 17 (dec) K1, p1, *k6, p1, k2tog, p1; rep from * to last 8 sts, k6, p1, sl 1, remove marker, sl 1 back to left needle, k2tog with first st of next rnd, pm—54 sts.

Rnd 18 *P1, k6, p1, k1; rep from * to end.

Rnd 19 (dec) P1, *k6, p3tog; rep from * to last 8 sts, k6, sl 2, remove marker, sl 2 back to LH needle, p3tog with first st of next rnd, pm—42 sts.

Rnd 20 *6-st LC, p1; rep from * to end.

Rnd 21 *K6, p1; rep from * to end.

Rnd 22 *[K2tog] 3 times, p1; rep from * to end—24 sts.

Rnd 23 [K2tog] 12 times—12 sts.

Rnd 24 [K2tog] 6 times—6 sts.

Break yarn, leaving a long tail. Draw tail through rem sts, pull tight and secure.

Finishing

With circular needle and RS facing, pick up and k 80 sts around lower edge of cable band. Pm for beg of rnd. Purl 1 rnd. Bind off purlwise.

Corkscrew tassel A

Cast on 15 sts.

Row 1 *Kfb; rep from * to end—30 sts.

Bind off.

Corkscrew tassel B (make 2)

Cast on 20 sts. Work as for tassel A.

Sew tassels to top of hat. ♣

Two Skeins

Intarsia Cowl

Intarsia Cowl

Oversize triangles in two colorways shaped with short rows add a modern, geometric vibe to this cowl.

Designed by Brenda Castiel

Skill Level:

■■■□

Materials

- 1 1¾oz/50g skein (each approx 110yd/100m) of Noro *Silk Garden* (silk/kid mohair/lambswool) each in #373 blue/sky/royal/light green (A) and #391 turquoise/sand/green/blue (B) ④
- One pair size 7 (4.5mm) needles OR SIZE TO OBTAIN GAUGE
- Size 7 (4.5mm) crochet hook
- Scrap yarn

Size
Instructions are written for one size.

Knitted Measurements
Circumference 25"/63.5cm
Width 9½"/24cm

Gauge
16 sts and 24 rows to 4"/10cm over St st using size 7 (4.5mm) needles. TAKE TIME TO CHECK GAUGE.

Stitch Glossary
RLI (right lifted inc) Insert tip of RH needle in the first leg of st below the next st on needle, place on LH needle and knit this st to inc 1 st.

Provisional Cast-On
With scrap yarn and crochet hook, ch the number of sts to cast on plus a few extra. Cut a tail and pull the tail through the last chain. With knitting needle and yarn, pick up and knit the stated number of sts through the "purl bumps" on the back of the chain. To remove scrap yarn chain, when instructed, pull out the tail from the last crochet stitch. Gently and slowly pull on the tail to unravel the crochet stitches, carefully placing each released knit stitch on a needle.

Short Row Wrap & Turn (w&t)
Knit (purl) side
1) Wyib, sl next st purlwise.
2) Move yarn between the needles to the front (back).
3) Sl the same st back to LH needle. Turn work, bring yarn to the knit (purl) side between needles. One st is wrapped.
4) When short rows are completed, hide all wraps as foll: work to just before wrapped st.
For knit side: Insert RH needle under the wrap and knitwise into the wrapped st, k them together.
For purl side: Insert RH needle from behind into the back loop of the wrap and place it on the LH needle; p wrap tog with st on needle.

Note
When changing colors, twist yarns on WS to prevent holes in work.

Cowl
First half
With B, cast on 44 sts using provisional cast-on.
Set-up row (RS) With B, sl 1, [p1, k1] 2 times, p1; join A, k to last 6 sts, [p1, k1] 3 times—6 B sts, 38 A sts.
Row 1 and all WS rows Sl 1, [k1, p1] 2 times, k1, p to last 6 sts, working sts in same color as previous row, [k1, p1] 3 times.

Row 2 With B, sl 1, [p1, k1] 2 times, p1, k1; with A, k to last 6 sts, [p1, k1] 3 times—7 B sts, 37 A sts.

Row 4 With B, sl 1, [p1, k1] 2 times, p1, RLI, k1; with A, k1, ssk, work in pat to end.

Row 6 With B, sl 1, [p1, k1] 2 times, p1, k1, RLI, k1; with A, k1, ssk, work in pat to end.

Row 8 With B, sl 1, [p1, k1] 2 times, p1, k to last 2 B sts, RLI, k2; with A, k1, ssk, work in pat to end.

Row 9 Rep row 1.

Rep rows 8 and 9 until 35 rows are complete—23 B sts, 21 A sts.

Begin short row shaping

Short row 1 (RS) Work 15 sts in pat, w&t, work to end.

Rows 36–41 Rep rows 8 and 9 three times.

Short row 2 Work 20 sts in pat, w&t, work to end.

Rows 42–47 Rep rows 8 and 9 three times.

Short row 3 Work 15 sts in pat, w&t, work to end.

Rows 48–53 Rep rows 8 and 9 three times.

Short row 4 Work 20 sts in pat, w&t, work to end.

Rows 54–59 Rep rows 8 and 9 three times.

Short row 5 Work 15 sts in pat, w&t; work to end.

Row 60 Rep row 8—36 B sts, 8 A sts.

Row 61 Rep row 9.

Row 62 Work in pat to last 2 B sts, RLI, k2; with A, ssk, work in pat to end.

Row 64 Work in pat to last 2 B sts, RLI, k1; with B, k2tog (B and A sts tog); with A, work in pat to end.

Second half

Row 1 (WS) With A, work in pat to last 6 sts; with B, work last 6 sts of ribbing.

Rows 2–64 Rep rows 2–64 as above.

Row 65 Rep row 1.

Finishing

Carefully undo provisional cast-on and place sts on needle. Graft ends tog using Kitchener st. ❖

Two Skeins

Picot Edge Shawlette

46

Picot Edge Shawlette

This simple-to-knit shawl looks anything but simple, with special details like buttons and an eyelet-and-picot border.

Designed by Cory Schrader

Skill Level:

■■□□

Materials

■ 2 1¾oz/50g skeins (each approx 136yd/124m) of Noro *Koromo* (cotton/wool/silk) each in #3 pumpkin/tan/cobalt/mint (**4**)
■ Size 6 (4mm) circular needle, 40"/101.5cm long, OR SIZE TO OBTAIN GAUGE
■ Two buttons, approx ⅞"/22mm diameter
■ Stitch markers

Size

Instructions are written for one size.

Knitted Measurements

Width 16"/40.5cm
Length 30"/76cm

Gauge

18 sts and 24 rows to 4"/10cm over St st using size 6 (4mm) needles.
TAKE TIME TO CHECK GAUGE.

Shawlette

Cast on 3 sts. Knit 6 rows. Pick up and k 3 sts along side edge and 3 sts along cast-on edge—9 sts.
Row 1 (WS) K3, p1, place marker (pm), p1 (center st), pm, p1, k3.
Row 2 K3, [yo, k1] 3 times, yo, k3—13 sts.
Row 3 K3, p to last 3 sts, k3.
Row 4 K3, yo, k to marker, yo, sl marker, k1, sl marker, yo, k to last 3 sts, yo, k3—4 sts inc'd.
Rep rows 3 and 4 until there are 101 sts, end with a WS row.
Next (buttonhole) row (RS) K3, [yo] 4 times, k to marker, yo, sl marker, k1, sl marker, yo, k to last 3 sts, yo, k3.
Next row K3, p to 4 yos; drop 3 loops off needle for buttonhole and p the last yo, k3.
Rep rows 3 and 4 until there are 145 sts, end with a WS row.
Next (buttonhole) row (RS) K3, [yo] 4 times, k3tog, k to 2 sts before marker, k2tog, yo, sl marker, k1, sl marker, yo, ssk, k to last 5 sts, k2tog, yo, k3—144 sts.
Next row K3, p to 4 yos; drop 3 loops off needle for buttonhole and p the last yo, k3.
Border
Row 1 K1, *yo, k2tog; rep from * to last st, yo, k1—145 sts.
Row 2 Purl.
Row 3 *K2tog, yo; rep from * to last st, k1.
Rep rows 2 and 3 five times more.
Picot bind-off
*Cast on 2 sts using cable cast-on method. Bind off 4 sts, place rem st back on LH needle; rep from * until all sts are bound off.

Finishing

Sew buttons opposite buttonholes. ❖

Three Skeins

Sinuous Cowl

Sinuous Cowl

Bands of garter stitch and ribbing undulate along a cowl that's a breeze to knit and to wear.

Designed by Alice Tang

Skill Level:

■■□□

Materials

- 3 3½oz/100g skeins (each approx 176yd/160m) of Noro *Obi* (silk/wool/mohair) in #7 pink/lilac/black/sky ⑤
- One pair size 8 (5mm) needles OR SIZE TO OBTAIN GAUGE
- Crochet hook and waste yarn for provisional cast-on

Size

Instructions are written for one size.

Knitted Measurements

Width 7½"/19cm
Length 60"/152.5cm

Gauge

14 sts and 25 rows to 4"/10cm over garter st using size 8 (5mm) needles. TAKE TIME TO CHECK GAUGE.

Stitch Glossary

Kfb Knit into the front and back of st—1 st increased.

Provisional Cast-On

Using scrap yarn and crochet hook, ch the number of sts to cast on plus a few extra. Cut a tail and pull the tail through the last chain. With knitting needle and yarn, pick up and knit the stated number of sts through the "purl bumps" on the back of the chain. To remove scrap yarn chain, when instructed, pull out the tail from the last crochet stitch. Gently and slowly pull on the tail to unravel the crochet stitches, carefully placing each released knit stitch on a needle.

3-Needle Bind-Off

1) Hold right sides of pieces together on 2 needles. Insert 3rd needle knitwise into first st of each needle, and wrap yarn knitwise.
2) Knit these 2 sts together, and slip them off the needles. *Knit the next 2 sts together in the same manner.
3) Slip first st on 3rd needle over 2nd st and off needle. Rep from * in step 2 across row until all sts are bound off.

Cowl

Using provisional cast-on, cast on 32 sts.
First straight section
Row 1 (RS) K14, [k1, p1] 9 times.
Row 2 [K1, p1] 9 times, k14.
Rep last 2 rows 12 times more.
**Right-leaning section
Row 1 K12, k2tog, [k1, p1] 8 times, k1, M1, p1.
Row 2 K1, [k1, p1] 9 times, k13.
Row 3 K11, k2tog, [k1, p1] 9 times, M1, k1.
Row 4 K2, [k1, p1] 9 times, k12.
Row 5 K10, k2tog, [k1, p1] 9 times, M1, k2.
Row 6 K3, [k1, p1] 9 times, k11.
Row 7 K9, k2tog, [k1, p1] 9 times, M1, k3.
Row 8 K4, [k1, p1] 9 times, k10.
Row 9 K8, k2tog, [k1, p1] 9 times, M1, k4.
Row 10 K5, [k1, p1] 9 times, k9.
Row 11 K7, k2tog, [k1, p1] 9 times, M1, k5.
Row 12 K6, [k1, p1] 9 times, k8.
Row 13 K6, k2tog, [k1, p1] 9 times, M1, k6.
Row 14 K7, [k1, p1] 9 times, k7.
Row 15 K5, k2tog, [k1, p1] 9 times, M1, k7.
Row 16 K8, [k1, p1] 9 times, k6.
Row 17 K4, k2tog, [k1, p1] 9 times, M1, k8.
Row 18 K9, [k1, p1] 9 times, k5.
Row 19 K3, k2tog, [k1, p1] 9 times, M1, k9.
Row 20 K10, [k1, p1] 9 times, k4.
Row 21 K2, k2tog, [k1, p1] 9 times, M1, k10.
Row 22 K11, [k1, p1] 9 times, k3.
Row 23 K1, k2tog, [k1, p1] 9 times, M1, k11.
Row 24 K12, [k1, p1] 9 times, k2.
Row 25 K2tog, [k1, p1] 9 times, M1, k12.

Row 26 K13, [k1, p1] 9 times, k1.
Row 27 K2tog, p1, [k1, p1] 8 times, M1, k13.
Row 28 K14, [k1, p1] 9 times.

Second straight section
Row 1 [K1, p1] 9 times, k14.
Row 2 K14, [k1, p1] 9 times.
Rep last 2 rows 25 times more.

Left-leaning section
Row 1 Kfb, p1, [k1, p1] 8 times, k2tog, k12.
Row 2 K13, [k1, p1] 9 times, k1.
Row 3 K1, M1, [k1, p1] 9 times, k2tog, k11.
Row 4 K12, [k1, p1] 9 times, k2.
Row 5 K2, M1, [k1, p1] 9 times, k2tog, k10.
Row 6 K11, [k1, p1] 9 times, k3.
Row 7 K3, M1, [k1, p1] 9 times, k2tog, k9.
Row 8 K10, [k1, p1] 9 times, k4.
Row 9 K4, M1, [k1, p1] 9 times, k2tog, k8.
Row 10 K9, [k1, p1] 9 times, k5.
Row 11 K5, M1, [k1, p1] 9 times, k2tog, k7.
Row 12 K8, [k1, p1] 9 times, k6.
Row 13 K6, M1, [k1, p1] 9 times, k2tog, k6.
Row 14 K7, [k1, p1] 9 times, k7.
Row 15 K7, M1, [k1, p1] 9 times, k2tog, k5.
Row 16 K6, [k1, p1] 9 times, k8.
Row 17 K8, M1, [k1, p1] 9 times, k2tog, k4.
Row 18 K5, [k1, p1] 9 times, k9.
Row 19 K9, M1, [k1, p1] 9 times, k2tog, k3.
Row 20 K4, [k1, p1] 9 times, k10.
Row 21 K10, M1, [k1, p1] 9 times, k2tog, k2.
Row 22 K3, [k1, p1] 9 times, k11.
Row 23 K11, M1, [k1, p1] 9 times, k2tog, k1.
Row 24 K2, [k1, p1] 9 times, k12.
Row 25 K12, M1, [k1, p1] 9 times, k2tog.
Row 26 K1, [k1, p1] 9 times, k13.
Row 27 K13, M1, [k1, p1] 8 times, k1, p2tog.
Row 28 [K1, p1] 9 times, k14.**

Third straight section
Row 1 K14, [k1, p1] 9 times.
Row 2 [K1, p1] 9 times, k14.
Rep last 2 rows 25 times more. Rep from ** to ** once more.

Fourth straight section
Row 1 (RS) K14, [k1, p1] 9 times.
Row 2 [K1, p1] 9 times, k14.
Rep last 2 rows 12 times more. Leave sts on needle.

Finishing
Carefully undo provisional cast-on and place sts on a 2nd needle, ready for a RS row—32 sts.
Join ends using 3-needle bind-off, being careful not to twist cowl.❖

One Skein

Lattice Cable Mitts

Lattice Cable Mitts

One bold color flows into the next as allover
latticework cables twist their way up these
fingerless gloves.

Designed by Cheryl Murray

Skill Level:
■■■□

Materials
- 1 1¾oz/50g skein (each approx 164yd/150m)
of Noro *Kirara* (wool/cotton/silk/angora) in #19
pink/orange/brown/turquoise (3)
- One set (4) size 3 (3.25mm) double-pointed needles
(dpns) OR SIZE TO OBTAIN GAUGE
- 2 each sizes 2 and 3 (2.5 and 3.25mm) circular
needles, 24"/60cm long
- Cable needle
- Stitch markers
- Scrap yarn

Size
Instructions are written for one size.

Knitted Measurements
Circumference 7½"/19cm
Length (wrist to top of middle finger) 8¼"/21cm

Gauge
28 sts and 40 rnds to 4"/10cm over chart pat using size 3 (3.25mm)
needles. TAKE TIME TO CHECK GAUGE.

Notes
1) The pattern is written for the body of the mitt to be worked using
two circular needles. The entire mitt can be worked using dpns if
desired.
2) Chart can be found on page 135.

Stitch Glossary
3-st RC Sl 2 sts to cn and hold to *back*, k1, k2 from cn.
3-st LC Sl 1 st to cn and hold to *front*, k2, k1 from cn.
M1R Insert LH needle from back to front under the strand between
last st worked and next st on LH needle. K into the front loop to
twist the st.
M1L Insert LH needle from front to back under the strand between
last st worked and next st on LH needle. K into the back loop to
twist the st.

Right Mitt
Cuff
With smaller needles, cast on 52 sts.
Divide sts on 2 circular needles, placing 27 sts on N1 and 25 sts on
N2. Place marker (pm) for beg of round and join, being careful not
to twist sts.
Rnd 1 *K1, p1; rep from * around for k1, p1 rib.
Rep rnd 1 until piece measures 2½"/6.5cm from beg. Change to
larger needles.
Beg chart
Next rnd Work row 1 of chart over the 27 sts on N1, k25 (for St st)
on N2. Cont to work chart in this manner for 2 rnds more.
Thumb gusset
Next (set-up) rnd On N1, cont in chart pat; on N2, k1, pm, k2, pm,
k to end.
Rnd 1 (inc) On N1, cont in chart pat; on N2, k1, sl marker, M1R, k to
2nd marker, M1L, sl marker, k to end—2 sts inc'd.
Rnds 2–3 Work even in pats as established.
Rep rnds 1–3 until there are 18 sts between markers.
Work even until piece measures 2½"/6.5cm from top of cuff.
Next rnd Work to first marker, remove marker. Place 18 gusset sts

on scrap yarn for thumb, cast on 2 sts, remove 2nd marker, work to end—52 sts.

Work even until piece measures 3¾"/9.5cm from top of cuff.

Little finger

Place first 6 sts on N1 and last 6 sts on N2 onto 3 dpns. Cast on 2 sts. Work in k1, p1 rib over 4 sts until finger measures 1¼"/3cm. Bind off in rib.

Rejoin yarn at base of little finger. Pm, pick up and k 2 sts along base of little finger, and work in k1, p1 rib over 42 sts for 2 rnds.

Ring finger

Next rnd Work to 6 sts before marker at base of little finger, place next 14 sts on dpns, cast on 2 sts—16 sts.

Work in k1, p1 rib until finger measures 1½"/4cm. Bind off in rib.

Middle finger

Place next 7 sts from N1 and N2 evenly on dpns. Join yarn, pick up and k 2 sts along base of ring finger—16 sts. Work in k1, p1 rib until finger measures 1¾"/4.5cm. Bind off in rib.

Index finger

Join yarn, pick up and k 2 sts along base of middle finger, knit rem 14 sts—16 sts.

Work in k1, p1 rib until finger measures 1½"/4cm from base. Bind off in rib.

Thumb

Place 18 gusset sts on dpns. Join yarn, pick up and k 3 sts along base of thumb—21 sts.

Work 7 rnds in k1, p1 rib. Bind off in rib.

Left Mitt

Work as for right glove to thumb gusset.

Thumb gusset

Set-up rnd Work to last 3 sts in rnd, pm, k2, pm, k1.

Rnd 1 Work to first marker, sl marker, M1R, k to 2nd marker, M1L, sl marker, work to end.

Rnds 2–3 Work even in pats as established.

Rep rnds 1–3 until there are 18 sts between markers.

Work even until piece measures 2½"/6.5cm from top of cuff. Work as for right glove to little finger.

Little finger

Work to last 6 sts on N1. Place last 6 sts on N1 and first 6 sts on N2 onto 3 dpns. Cast on 2 sts—14 sts.

Work in k1, p1 rib until finger measures 1¼"/3cm. Bind off in rib.

Complete as for right glove. ❖

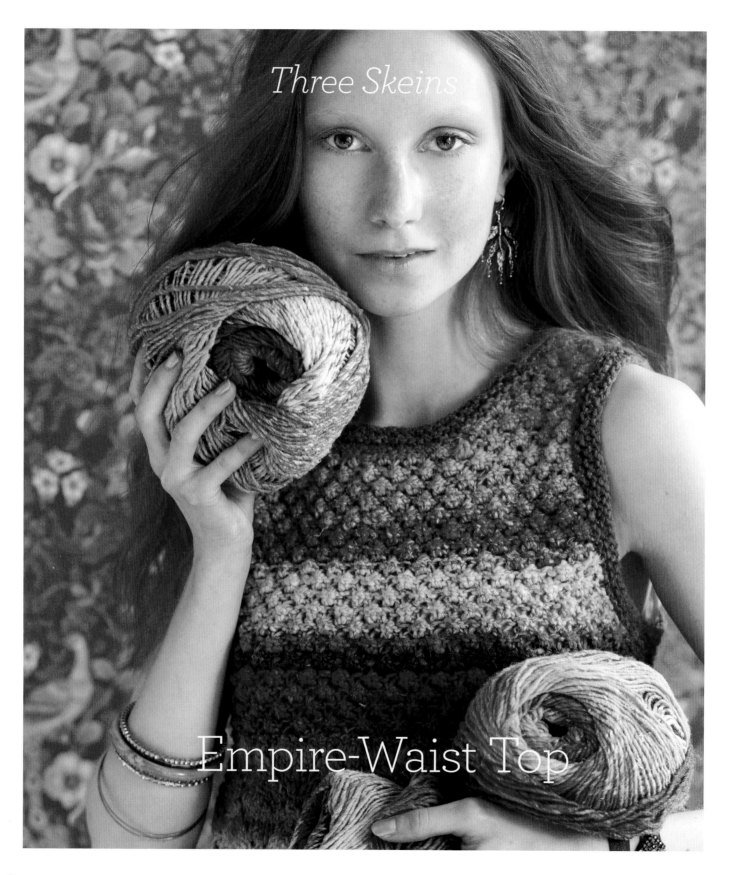

Three Skeins

Empire-Waist Top

Empire-Waist Top

The textured bodice and lacy bottom half help this sweet top achieve both structure and lightness.

Designed by Mari Tobita

Skill Level:

■■■□

Materials

- 3 (4, 5) 3½oz/100g skeins (each approx 218yd/200m) of Noro *Taiyo* (cotton/silk/wool/nylon) in #48 pink/violet/sienna (4)
- One each size 8 (5mm) circular needles, 16 and 32"/40 and 81cm long, OR SIZE TO OBTAIN GAUGE
- Stitch holders
- Stitch markers

Sizes

Instructions are written for size Small. Changes for Medium and Large are in parentheses. (Shown in size Small.)

Knitted Measurements

Bust 35½ (40, 44½)"/90 (101.5, 113)cm
Length 21 (21¼, 22)"/53.5 (54.5, 56)cm

Gauge

18 sts and 22 rows to 4"/10cm over bubble pat using size 8 (5mm) needles. TAKE TIME TO CHECK GAUGE.

.3-Needle Bind-Off

1) Hold right sides of pieces together on 2 needles. Insert 3rd needle knitwise into first st of each needle, and wrap yarn knitwise.
2) Knit these 2 sts together, and slip them off the needles. *Knit the next 2 sts together in the same manner.
3) Slip 1st st on 3rd needle over 2nd st and off needle. Rep from * in step 2 across row until all sts are bound off.

Lace Pattern

Note When working rnds 2, 4, 6, and 16, work to marker, remove marker, k1, place marker (pm) for new beg of rnd.
Rnd 1 *K3, yo, k1, yo, k3, SK2P; rep from * around.
Rnd 2 and all even-numbered rnds Knit.
Rnd 3 *K2, yo, k3, yo, k2, SK2P; rep from * around.
Rnd 5 *K1, yo, k5, yo, k1, SK2P; rep from * around.
Rnd 7 *Yo, k7, yo, SK2P; rep from * around.
Rnd 9 *Yo, k3, SK2P, k3, yo, k1; rep from * around.
Rnd 11 *K1, yo, k2, SK2P, k2, yo, k2; rep from * around.
Rnd 13 *K2, yo, k1, SK2P, k1, yo, k3; rep from * around.
Rnd 15 *K3, yo, SK2P, yo, k4; rep from * around.
Rnd 16 Knit.
Rep rnds 1–16 for lace pat.

Bubble Pattern

(multiple of 4 sts, worked in rnds)
Rnds 1 and 3 Purl.
Rnd 2 *K3tog, [p1, k1, p1] in same st; rep from * around.
Rnd 4 *[P1, k1, p1] in same st, k3tog; rep from * around.
Rep rnds 1–4 for bubble pat in rnds.

Bubble Pattern

(multiple of 4 plus 2, worked in rows)
Rows 1 and 3 (RS) K1, p to last st, k1.
Row 2 K1, *[k1, p1, k1] in same st, p3tog; rep from * to last st, k1.
Row 4 K1, *p3tog, [k1, p1, k1] in same st; rep from * to last st, k1.
Rep rnds 1–4 for bubble pat in rows.

Note

Body is worked in one piece to armholes.

Body

With longer circular needle, cast on 180 (200, 220) sts. Pm for beg of rnd and join, being careful not to twist sts. Purl 1 rnd.
Begin lace pat
Work in lace pat until piece measures 11"/28cm from beg.
Next rnd Purl, dec 20 sts evenly around—160 (180, 200) sts.
Begin bubble pat
Work rnds 2–4 of bubble pat in rnds, then rep rows 1–4 until piece measures 13"/33cm from beg, end with a rnd 1 or 3.

Divide for front and back
Next rnd P80 (90, 100), pm for side, p to end of rnd.
Next row (RS) Bind off 4 (5, 7) sts, work in bubble pat as established to marker, turn.
Next row Bind off 4 (5, 7) sts at beg of row, work in pat to end. Cont on these sts for back; place rem 80 (90, 100) sts on hold for front.

Back
Armhole shaping
Cont in bubble pat as established, bind off 3 sts at beg of next 2 (2, 4) rows, bind off 2 sts at beg of next 2 rows, bind off 1 st at beg of next 4 rows—58 (62, 66) sts. Work even in pat until armhole measures 6¾ (7¼, 7¾)"/17 (18.5, 19.5)cm, end with a WS row.
Neck shaping
Next row (RS) Work 20 (22, 24) sts in pat, join a 2nd ball of yarn and bind off center 18 sts, work to end of row.
Working both sides at once, bind off 10 sts at each neck edge once—10 (12, 14) sts each side. Work even until armhole measures 7½ (8, 8½)"/19 (20.5, 21.5)cm. Place sts on holder.

Front
Place sts for front on needle ready to work a RS row. Bind off 4 (5, 7) sts at beg of next 2 rows. Work as for back until armhole measures 4½ (5, 5½)"/11.5 (12.5, 14)cm, end with a WS row.
Neck shaping
Next row (RS) Cont in bubble pat as established, work 23 (25, 27) sts, join a 2nd ball of yarn and bind off center 12 sts, work to end of row.
Working both sides at once, bind off from each neck edge 4 sts once, 3 sts twice, 2 sts once, then 1 st once—10 (12, 14) sts each side. Work even until armholes measure same as back.

Finishing
Block pieces to measurements. Join shoulder seams using 3-needle bind-off method.
Neckband
With shorter circular needle and RS facing, pick up and k 82 sts around neck opening, pm for beg of rnd. Work 4 rnds in garter st. Bind off purlwise.
Sew side seams.
Armhole band
With shorter circular needle and RS facing, pick up and k 78 (82, 86) sts around armhole opening, pm for beg of rnd. Complete as for neckband. ❦

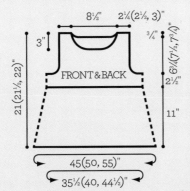

8½"   2¼(2½, 3)"

¾"

3"

FRONT & BACK

6¾(7½, 7¾)"

2½"

21 (21¼, 22)"

11"

45(50, 55)"

35½(40, 44½)"

Three Skeins

Lace Pillow Sham

Lace Pillow Sham

This homey pillow cover features columns of lace that evoke cables, along with an elegantly shaped button flap.

Designed by Ellen Liguori

Skill Level:

■■■□

Materials

- 3 1¾oz/50g skeins (each approx 110yd/100m) of Noro *Kureyon* (wool) in #272 red/purple/mint/yellow ④
- One pair size 10 (6mm) needles OR SIZE TO OBTAIN GAUGE
- Size H/8 (5mm) crochet hook
- Five buttons
- Stitch markers
- One pillow form, 12 x 16"/30.5 x 40.5cm

Knitted Measurements

Width 12"/30.5cm
Length 16"/40.5cm

Gauge

14 sts and 22 rows to 4"/10cm over pat st using size 10 (6mm) needles. TAKE TIME TO CHECK GAUGE.

Stitch Glossary

ch Crochet chain st.
sc Single crochet.

Seed Stitch

(over an odd number of sts)
Row 1 (RS) *K1, p1; rep from *, end k1.
Row 2 K the purl sts and p the knit sts.
Rep row 2 for seed st.

Note

Cover is worked from the flap down in one piece, folded and seamed at the sides.

Pillow Sham

Cast on 15 sts.
Row 1 (RS) Purl.
Row 2 K1, p13, k1.
Row 3 P1, k1, p11, k1, p1.
Row 4 K1, p1, k11, p1, k1.
Row 5 P1, k1, p2, k2tog, [k1, yo] twice, k1, SKP, p2, k1, p1.
Row 6 K1, p1, k2, p7, k2, p1, k1.
Row 7 P1, k1, p2, k2tog, yo, k3, yo, SKP, p2, k1, p1.
Row 8 Rep row 6.
Row 9 Cast on 12 sts, p13, k1, p2, k1, yo, SKP, k1, k2tog, yo, k1, p2, k1, p1—27 sts.
Row 10 Cast on 12 sts, k1, p11, k1, p1, k2, p7, k2, p1, k1, p11, k1—39 sts.
Row 11 P1, k1, p11, k1, p2, k2, yo, SK2P, yo, k2, p2, k1, p11, k1, p1.
Row 12 K1, p1, k11, p1, k2, p7, k2, p1, k11, p1, k1.
Row 13 P1, k1, *p2, k2tog, [k1, yo] twice, k1, SKP, p2, k1; rep from * to last st, p1.
Row 14 K1, p1, *k2, p7, k2, p1; rep from * to last st, k1.
Row 15 P1, k1, *p2, k2tog, yo, k3, yo, SKP, p2, k1; rep from * to last st, p1.
Row 16 Rep row 14.
Row 17 Cast on 12 sts, p13, k1, *p2, k1, yo, SKP, k1, k2tog, yo, k1, p2, k1; rep from * to last st, p1—51 sts.
Row 18 Cast on 12 sts, k1, p11, k1, p1, *k2, p7, k2, p1, rep from * to last 13 sts, k1, p11, k1—63 sts.
Row 19 P1, k1, p11, k1, *p2, k2, yo, sk2p, yo, k2, p2, k1; rep from * to last 13 sts, p11, k1, p1.

Row 20 K1, p11, k1, p1, *k2, p7, k2, p1, rep from * to last 13 sts, k1, p11, k1.

Row 21 P1, k1, *p2, k2tog, [k1, yo] twice, SKP, p2, k1; rep from * to last st, p1.

Rows 22, 24, and 26 K1, p1, *k2, p7, k2, p1; rep from * to last st, k1.

Row 23 P1, k1, *p2, k2tog, yo, k3, yo, SKP, p2, k1; rep from * to last st, p1.

Row 25 P1, k1, *p2, k1, yo, SKP, k1, k2tog, yo, k1, p2, k1; rep from * to last st, p1.

Row 27 P1, k1, *p2, k2, yo, sk2p, yo, k2, p2, k1; rep from * to last st, p1.

Row 28 K1, p1, *k2, p7, k2, p1; rep from * to last st, k1.

Rep rows 21–28 fifteen times more.

Work 4 rows in seed st, end with a WS row. Bind off in pat.

Finishing

Flap trim

Place a marker in the cast-on edges of the flap to correspond to the center stitch of each lace diamond—5 sts marked. With crochet hook and RS facing, join yarn with a sl st in RH side of cast-on edge. Ch 1, [sc in each st to marked st, (sc, ch 5, sc) in next st (button loop made), sc in next 4 sts, 4 sc evenly along side edge of "step," 2 sc in corner] twice, [sc in each st to marked st, make button loop on marked st, sc in each st to corner, 2 sc in corner, 4 sc evenly along side edge of "step"] 3 times. Fasten off.

Place markers 20"/51cm up from bound-off edge along sides. With WS together, fold bound-off edge to marker and sew side seams. Insert pillow form and fold top edge over. Mark position for five buttons opposite button loops. Sew on buttons. ♣

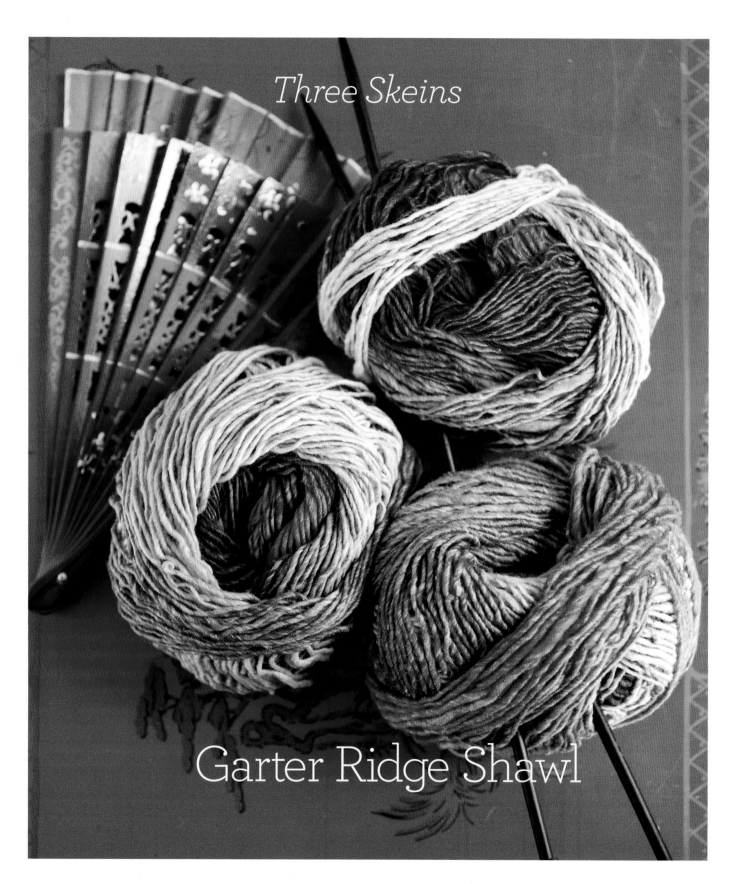

Three Skeins

Garter Ridge Shawl

Garter Ridge Shawl

Single-row garter ridges help emphasize the striking color changes and subtle shaping in this design.

Designed by Rachel Roden

Skill Level:
■■□□

Materials
- 2 1³⁄₄oz/50g skeins (each approx 136yd/124m) of Noro *Koromo* (cotton/wool/silk) each in #3 pumpkin/tan/cobalt/mint (4)
- Size 6 (4mm) circular needle, 40"/101.5cm long, OR SIZE TO OBTAIN GAUGE
- Two buttons, approx ⁷⁄₈"/22mm diameter
- Stitch markers

Size
Instructions are written for one size.

Knitted Measurements
Width at widest point (after blocking) 22"/56cm
Length (after blocking) 58"/147cm

Gauge
18 sts and 24 rows to 4"/10cm over St st using size 6 (4mm) needles, after blocking. TAKE TIME TO CHECK GAUGE.

Shawl
Cast on 3 sts. Knit 8 rows. Pick up and k 4 sts along side edge and 3 sts along cast-on edge—10 sts.

Section 1
Row 1 (WS) K3, place marker (pm), p4, pm, k3.
Row 2 K3, sl marker, [M1, k1] 4 times, M1, sl marker, k3—15 sts.
Row 3 K3, purl to last 3 sts, k3.
Row 4 K3, sl marker, [M1, k1, M1, pm, k1, pm] 4 times, M1, k1, M1, sl marker, k3—25 sts.
Rows 5 and 6 Knit.
Row 7 K3, purl to last 3 sts, k3.
Row 8 (inc) K3, sl marker, [M1, k to marker, M1, sl marker, k1, sl marker] 4 times, M1, knit to marker, M1, sl marker, k3—10 sts inc'd.
Rows 9 and 10 Knit.
Row 11 K3, purl to last 3 sts, k3.
Rows 12–35 Rep rows 8–11 six times—95 sts.

Section 2
Row 36 Rep row 8 (inc row)—105 sts.
Row 37 K3, purl to last 3 sts, k3.
Rows 38–40 Knit.
Row 41 K3, purl to last 3 sts, k3.
Rows 42–71 Rep rows 36–41 five times—155 sts.

Section 3
Row 72 Rep row 8 (inc row)—165 sts.
Row 73 K3, purl to last 3 sts, k3.
Row 74 Knit.
Row 75 K3, purl to last 3 sts, k3.
Rows 76–78 Knit.
Row 79 K3, purl to last 3 sts, k3.
Rows 80–111 Rep rows 72–79 four times—205 sts.
Rows 112–117 Rep rows 72–77—215 sts. Remove all markers.

Section 4
Row 118 K3, k2tog, *yo, sl 1, k2, pass the sl st over the k2; rep from * to marker, k3—214 sts.
Row 119 K3, purl to last 3 sts, k3.
Row 120 K3, *sl 1, k2, pass the sl st over the k2, yo; rep from * to 1 st before marker, k4.
Row 121 K3, purl to last 3 sts, k3.
Rep rows 118–121 three times more.

Picot bind-off
Bind off as foll: *Cast on 2 sts using the cable cast-on method, bind off 5 sts, sl rem st back to LH needle; rep from * until all sts have been bound off. ❧

Three Skeins

Bias-Knit Scarf

Bias-Knit Scarf

The bold diagonal lines of this scarf knit on the bias are enhanced by garter ridge stripes.

Designed by Betty Balcomb

Skill Level:

■■☐☐

Materials

- 3 1¾oz/50g skeins (each approx 110yd/100m) of Noro *Silk Garden* (silk/mohair/wool) in #357 orange/violet/turquoise (4)
- One pair size 9 (5.5mm) needles OR SIZE TO OBTAIN GAUGE

Size

Instructions are written for one size.

Knitted Measurements

Width 7"/18cm
Length 68"/173cm

Gauge

15 sts and 26 rows to 4"/10cm over pat st using size 9 (5.5mm) needles. TAKE TIME TO CHECK GAUGE.

Stitch Glossary

kfb Knit into the front and back of st—1 st increased.

Pattern Stitch

(over any number of sts)
Rows 1 and 3 (RS) With A, kfb, k to last 2 sts, k2tog.
Rows 2 and 4 With A, knit.
Row 5 With B, kfb, k to last 2 sts, k2tog.
Row 6 With B, purl.
Rep rows 1–6 for pat st.

Notes

1) Before beginning, designate 2 skeins as A and 1 skein as B. Make sure that the B skein starts in a different place in the color sequence than the first A skein.
2) Carry yarn not in use along side edge.

Scarf

With A, cast on 2 sts.
Row 1 (RS) Kfb, k1—3 sts.
Row 2 Kfb, k2—4 sts.
Rows 3–6 With A, kfb, k to end of row—8 sts.
Row 7 With B, kfb, k to last 2 sts, kfb, k1—10 sts.
Row 8 With B, purl.
Rep rows 3–8 five times more, end with WS row—40 sts.
Begin pat st
Work in pat st until piece measures approx 57"/145cm from beg, end with a row 6.
Next row (RS) With A, ssk, k to last 2 sts, k2tog—38 sts.
Next row With A, knit.
Next 2 rows Rep last 2 rows once more—36 sts.
Next row With B, ssk, k to last 2 sts, k2tog—34 sts.
Next row With B, purl.
Rep last 6 rows 4 times more—10 sts.
Next row (RS) With A, ssk, k to last 2 sts, k2tog—6 sts.
Next row With A, knit.
Rep last 2 rows once more—4 sts.
Next row [K2tog] twice, pass 1st st on RH needle over 2nd st and fasten off. ❧

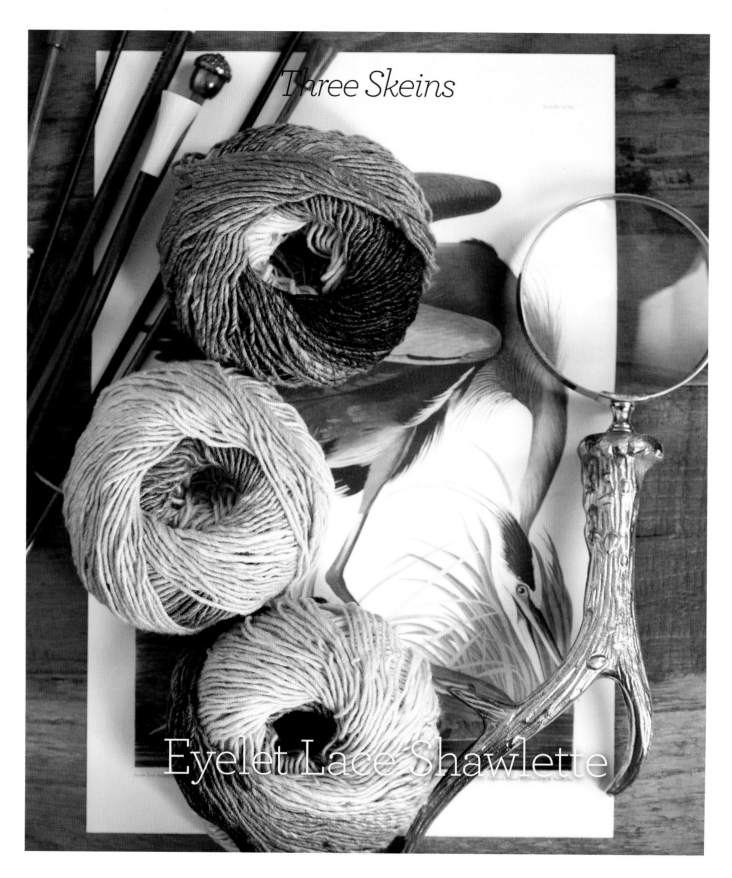

Three Skeins

Eyelet Lace Shawlette

Eyelet Lace Shawlette

A subtle crescent shape and pretty eyelets make a feminine wrap that can be worn a multitude of ways.

Designed by Cheryl Murray

Skill Level:
■■■□

Materials
- 3 1¾oz/50g skeins (each approx 137yd/125m) of Noro *Shiro* (wool/cashmere/silk) in #2 grey/sand/turquoise (3)
- Size 10 (6mm) circular needle, 32"/81cm long, OR SIZE TO OBTAIN GAUGE

Size
Instructions are written for one size.

Knitted Measurements
Width at widest point 10"/25.5cm
Length 78"/198cm

Gauge
13 sts and 20 rows to 4"/10cm over horizontal eyelet pat using size 10 (6mm) needles. TAKE TIME TO CHECK GAUGE.

Stitch Glossary
PUK Pick up wrap and knit together with wrapped st.
PUP Pick up wrap and purl together with wrapped st.

Short Row Wrap & Turn (w&t)
On RS row (on WS row)
1) Wyib (wyif), sl next st purlwise.
2) Move yarn between the needles to the front (back).
3) Sl the same st back to LH needle. Turn work. One st is wrapped.
4) When working the wrapped st, insert RH needle under the wrap and work it tog with the corresponding st on needle (PUK/PUP).

Notes
1) Circular needle is used to accommodate large number of sts. Do not join.
2) Charts can be found on page 135.

Shawlette
Cast on 248 sts. Purl 2 rows.
Begin vertical eyelet chart
Setup row (WS) P2, *k1, p2, rep from * to end.
Next row (RS) Work 6-st rep of vertical eyelet chart 41 times across, work to end of chart.
Cont to work chart in this manner until row 4 is complete. Rep rows 1–4 of vertical eyelet chart twice more. Knit 2 rows.
Begin short row pattern and horizontal eyelet chart
Working short rows as foll, rep rows 1–10 of horizontal eyelet chart 3 times, then rep rows 1–6 once more:
Short row 1 (RS) K129, w&t.
Short row 2 (WS) P10, w&t.
Short row 3 Work to wrap, PUK, k4, w&t.
Short row 4 Work to wrap, PUP, p4, w&t.
Rep short rows 3 and 4 for 8 times more.
Next row (RS) Knit to wrap, PUK, k7, w&t.
Next row Purl to wrap, PUP, p7, w&t.
Rep last 2 rows 4 times more.
Next row (RS) Knit to wrap, PUK, k9, w&t.
Next row Purl to wrap, PUP, p9, w&t.
Rep last 2 rows twice more.
Knit 2 rows across all sts. Bind off loosely. ❧

One Skein

Twisted Rib Beanie

Twisted Rib Beanie

A pattern of alternating ribs and eyelets exudes warmth and drama in rich hues of aran-weight yarn.

Designed by Lisa Craig

Skill Level:
■■■□

Materials

- 1 3½oz/100g hank (each approx 197yd/180m) of Noro *Cyochin* (wool/silk/mohair) in #2 grape/blue/pink/black (4)
- One set (5) each size 7 and 8 (4.5 and 5mm) double-pointed needles (dpns) OR SIZE TO OBTAIN GAUGE

Size

Instructions are written for one size.

Knitted Measurements

Circumference 17"/43cm
Length 8"/20.5cm

Gauge

20 sts and 24 rows to 4"/10cm over twisted rib and eyelet pat using size 8 (5mm) needles. TAKE TIME TO CHECK GAUGE.

Twisted Rib and Eyelet Pattern

Rnds 1–4 *K4 tbl, p2, k3 tbl, p2; rep from * around.
Rnd 5 *K4 tbl, p1, k2tog, yo, k1 tbl, yo, SKP, p1; rep from * around.
Rnd 6 *K4 tbl, p1, [k1 tbl, k1] twice, k1 tbl, p1; rep from * around.
Rnds 7–10 Rep rnds 1 and 2 twice.
Rep rnds 1–10 for twisted rib and eyelet pat.

Hat

With smaller needles, cast on 88 sts. Divide sts evenly on 4 dpns. Pm for beg of rnd and join, being careful not to twist sts.
Work rnds 1–4 of twisted rib and eyelet pat.
Change to larger needles. Cont in twisted rib and eyelet pat until rnd 10 is complete, rep rnds 1–10 twice more, then rnds 1–4 once. Piece measures approx 6"/15cm from beg.

Crown shaping

Rnd 1 *K4 tbl, p2tog, k3 tbl, p2tog; rep from * around—72 sts.
Rnd 2 *K4 tbl, p1, k3 tbl, p1; rep from * around.
Rnd 3 *K2tog tbl, k2 tbl, p1, k2tog tbl, k1 tbl, p1; rep from * around—56 sts.
Rnd 4 *K3 tbl, p1, k2 tbl, p1; rep from * around.
Rnd 5 *K2tog tbl, k1 tbl, p1, k2 tbl, p1; rep from * around—48 sts.
Rnd 6 *K2 tbl, p1; rep from * around.
Rnd 7 *K2tog tbl, p1; rep from * around—32 sts.
Rnd 8 *K1 tbl, p1; rep from * around.
Rnd 9 [K2tog tbl] 16 times—16 sts.
Rnd 10 [K2tog tbl] 8 times—8 sts.
Cut yarn, draw through rem sts, pull tight and secure. ❖

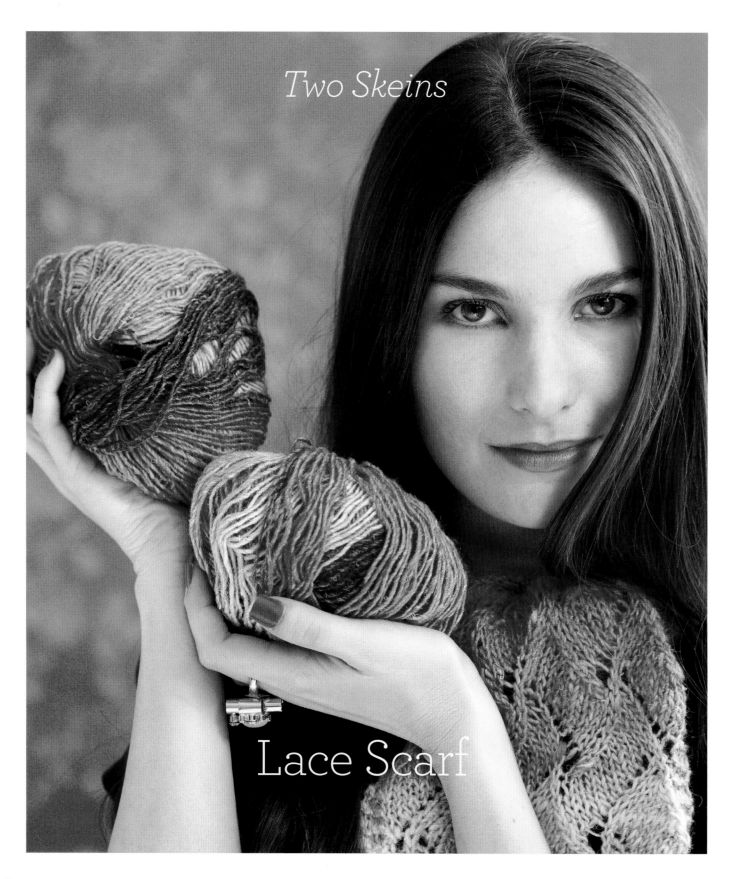

Two Skeins

Lace Scarf

Lace Scarf

Softly undulating eyelets are the perfect complement to the subtle transitions of this *Silk Garden Lite* colorway.

Designed by Carol J. Sulcoski

Skill Level:
■■■□

Materials
- 2 1¾oz/50g skeins (each approx 137yd/125m) of Noro *Silk Garden Lite* (silk/kid mohair/lambswool) in #2094 silver/green/orange/pink ③
- One pair size 7 (4.5mm) needles OR SIZE TO OBTAIN GAUGE
- Spare size 7 (4.5mm) needle

Size
Instructions are written for one size.

Knitted Measurements
Width (after blocking) 7½"/19cm
Length (after blocking) 45"/114cm

Gauge
19 sts and 28 rows to 4"/10cm over swirling lace pat using size 7 (4.5mm) needles. TAKE TIME TO CHECK GAUGE.

Note
Each half of scarf is worked from end to center, and then pieces are joined.

Swirling Lace Pattern
(multiple of 10 sts)
Row 1 (RS) *Yo, k8, k2tog; rep from * across.
Row 2 *P2tog, p7, yo, p1; rep from * across.
Row 3 *K2, yo, k6, k2tog; rep from * across.
Row 4 *P2tog, p5, yo, p3; rep from * across.
Row 5 *K4, yo, k4, k2tog; rep from * across.
Row 6 *P2tog, p3, yo, p5; rep from * across.
Row 7 *K6, yo, k2, k2tog; rep from * across.
Row 8 *P2tog, p1, yo, p7; rep from * across.
Row 9 *K8, yo, k2tog; rep from * across.
Row 10 *Yo, p8, p2tog tbl; rep from * across.
Row 11 *Ssk, k7, yo, k1; rep from * across.
Row 12 *P2, yo, p6, p2tog tbl; rep from * across.
Row 13 *Ssk, k5, yo, k3; rep from * across.
Row 14 *P4, yo, p4, p2tog tbl; rep from * across.
Row 15 *Ssk, k3, yo, k5; rep from * across.
Row 16 *P6, yo, p2, p2tog tbl; rep from * across.
Row 17 *Ssk, k1, yo, k7; rep from * across.
Row 18 *P8, yo, p2tog tbl; rep from * across.
Rep rows 1–18 for swirling lace pat.

3-Needle Bind-Off
1) Hold right sides of pieces together on two needles. Insert third needle knitwise into first st of each needle, and wrap yarn knitwise.
2) Knit these two sts together, and slip them off the needles. *Knit the next two sts together in the same manner.
3) Slip first st on 3rd needle over 2nd st and off needle. Rep from * in step 2 across row until all sts are bound off.

Scarf
First half
Cast on 36 sts. Knit 4 rows.
Row 1 (RS) K3, work 10-st rep of swirling lace pat 3 times across, k3.
Row 2 K3, work 10-st rep of swirling lace pat 3 times across, k3.
Cont in this manner, knitting first and last 3 sts of every row, until row 18 is complete. Rep rows 1–18 for 6 times more. Knit 2 rows.
Place sts for first half on spare needle.
Second half
Work as for first half, leaving sts on needle when complete.

Finishing
Graft 2 halves together using Kitchener st or 3-needle bind-off.
Block lightly to open lace. ✤

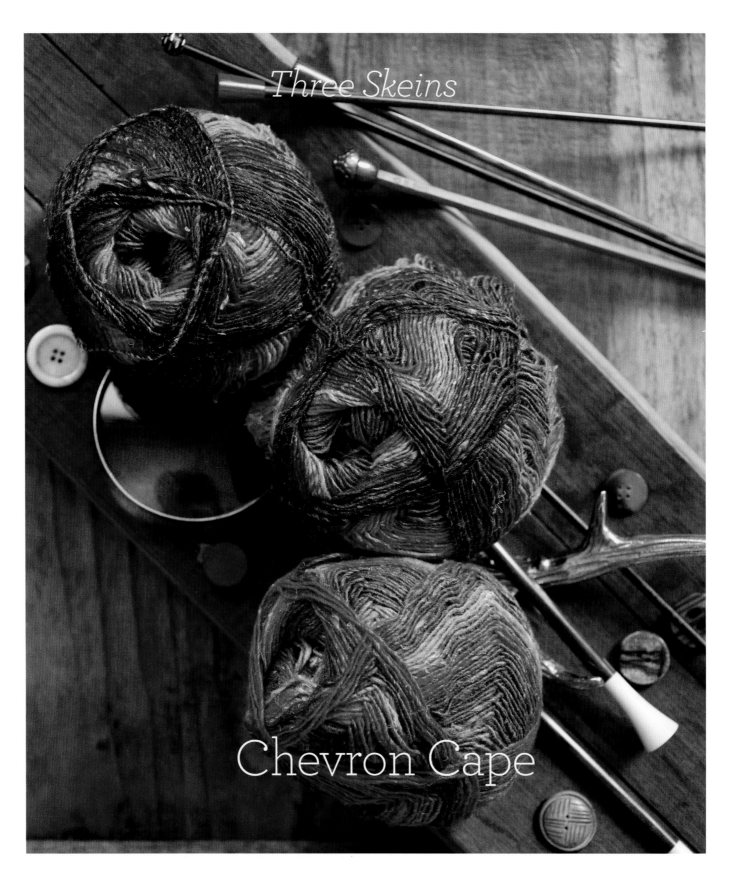

Three Skeins

Chevron Cape

Chevron Cape

With thw warm hues and rustic textures of this cape, you'll welcome the chill of autumn.

Designed by Therese Chynoweth

Skill Level:

■■■□

Materials

- 3 3½oz/100g skeins (each approx 328yd/300m) of Noro *Silk Garden Sock* (lamb/silk/nylon/kid mohair) in #349 burnt orange/wine/grey/taupe (2)
- Size 5 (3.75mm) circular needle, 32"/81.5cm long, OR SIZE TO OBTAIN GAUGE
- One set (5) size 5 (3.75mm) double-pointed needles (dpns)
- 3 buttons, approx 1⅝"/41mm diameter
- Scrap yarn

Size

Instructions are written for one size.

Knitted Measurements

Width approx 51"/129.5cm
Length approx 15½"/39.5cm

Gauge

22 sts and 32 rows to 4"/10cm over chart 1 pat using size 5 (3.75mm) needles. TAKE TIME TO CHECK GAUGE.

Stitch Glossary

MB (make bobble) Knit into front, back, then front of next st (3 sts made from 1), turn; p3, turn; k3, pass 1st and 2nd sts over 3rd st and off needle—1 st.
LT (left twist) Sl 2 sts knitwise, 1 at a time, place both sts back on LH needle in new orientation, k 2nd st tbl, k2tog tbl, sl both sts from LH needle.
RT (right twist) K2tog but do not remove from LH needle, k 2nd st again, sl both sts from LH needle.
Ssp (slip, slip, purl) Wyif, sl 2 sts knitwise 1 at a time to RH needle. Sl them back to LH needle and p2tog tbl.

Left Pleat

(worked over 48 sts)
Sl next 16 sts to first dpn (N1), sl next 16 sts to 2nd dpn (N2), hold dpns to outside with RS of N2 next to RS of LH needle, and WS of N1 over top of N2. *With RH needle, knit tog 1 st from each needle (k3tog); rep from * until all pleat sts have been worked—32 sts dec.

Right Pleat

(worked over 48 sts)
Sl next 16 sts to first dpn (N1), sl next 16 sts to 2nd dpn (N2), hold dpns to inside with WS of N2 next to WS of LH needle, and RS of N1 under N2. *With RH needle, knit tog 1 st from each needle (k3tog); rep from * until all pleat sts have been worked—32 sts dec.

One-Row Buttonhole

Work to button placement; wyif, sl 1 purlwise; wyib, *sl next st purlwise, bind off st (by passing first slipped st over 2nd slipped st); rep from * 5 times total. Place last bound-off st back on LH needle. Turn work to WS and, wyib, cast on 6 sts using the cable cast-on method. Turn work to RS and, wyib, slip 1 purlwise and pass the last cast-on st over the slipped st.

Notes
1) A circular needle is used to accommodate the large number of stitches. Do not turn.
2) Charts can be found on page 136.

Cape
Cast on 281 sts. Knit 1 row.
Next row Sl 1 wyif, k to end.
Rep last row 6 times more.
Begin chart 1
Row 1 (RS) Sl 1 wyif, k13, work 39-st rep of chart row 6 times across, work to end of chart, k14.
Next row Sl 1 wyif, k13, work to rep line, work 39-st rep of chart row 6 times across, k14.
Cont to work chart 1 in this manner until row 16 is complete. Rep rows 1–16 until piece measures 10½"/26.5 cm from beg, end with a WS row.
Next (buttonhole) row (RS) Sl 1 wyif, k5, work one-row buttonhole over next 5 sts, work to end in pat.
Cont in pat until piece measures 13½"/34.5cm from beg, end with a WS row. Rep buttonhole row. Cont in pat until piece measures 15"/38cm from beg, end with a WS row. Do not break yarn. Place sts on scrap yarn and block lightly to measurements.

Collar
Place sts back on circular needle.
Next row (RS) K25, right pleat, k10, left pleat, k19, right pleat, k10, left pleat, k25—153 sts.
Knit 5 rows, slipping first st of every row.
Next (dec) row (RS) Sl 1 wyif, k13, [k6, k2tog] 15 times, k to end—138 sts.
Next row Sl 1 wyif, k to end.
Next (dec) row Sl 1 wyif, k5, work buttonhole over next 5 sts, k9, [ssk, k6, k2tog, k12] 5 times, k to end—128 sts.
Begin chart 2
Next row (WS) Sl 1 wyif, k13, work row 2 of chart 2, working 20-st rep 5 times across, k to end.
Cont to work chart 2 in this manner until row 16 is complete. Work rows 1–11 once. Bind off knitwise.

Finishing
Sew on buttons opposite buttonholes. ❧

One Skein

Flower Brooch

Flower Brooch

The rich hues of a soft blend that includes cashmere and angora are shown off in the spiraling petals of a flower.

Designed by Jacqueline Van Dillen

Skill Level:
■■□□

Materials
- 1 1¾oz/50g hank (each approx 198yd/181m) of Noro *Shiraito* (cashmere/angora/wool) in #34 orange/turquoise/cocoa/blue 🧶**1**
- One pair size 4 (3.5mm) needles (dpns) OR SIZE TO OBTAIN GAUGE
- Pin back

Knitted Measurements
Height approx 2¼"/5.5cm
Diameter approx 3"/7.5cm

Gauge
22 sts and 44 rows to 4"/10cm over garter st using size 4 (3.5mm) needles. TAKE TIME TO CHECK GAUGE.

Leaves (make 2)
Cast on 3 sts.
Row 1 (RS) K1, k1 tbl, k1.
Rows 2 and 26 K1, p1, k1.
Row 3 K1, M1, k1 tbl, M1, k1—5 sts.
Rows 4 and 24 K2, p1, k2.
Row 5 K2, M1, k1 tbl, M1, k2—7 sts.
Rows 6 and 22 K3, p1, k3.
Row 7 K3, M1, k1 tbl, M1, k3—9 sts.
Rows 8 and 20 K4, p1, k4.
Row 9 K4, M1, k1 tbl, M1, k4—11 sts.
Rows 10 and 18 K5, p1, k5.
Row 11 K5, M1, k1 tbl, M1, k5—13 sts.
Rows 12 and 16 K6, p1, k6.
Row 13 K6, M1, k1 tbl, M1, k6—15 sts.
Row 14 K7, p1, k7.
Row 15 K6, SK2P, k6—13 sts.
Row 17 K5, SK2P, k5—11 sts.
Row 19 K4, SK2P, k4—9 sts.
Row 21 K3, SK2P, k3—7 sts.
Row 23 K2, SK2P, k2—5 sts.
Row 25 K1, SK2P, k1—3 sts.
Row 27 SK2P—1 st. Fasten off.

Flower
Cast on 3 sts. Knit 4 rows.
Next (inc) row (RS) Knit to last st, M1, k1—4 sts.
Cont in garter st (knit every row) and rep inc row every 4th row 5 times more, then every 8th row 4 times—13 sts. Work even in garter st until piece measures 12"/30.5cm from beg, end with a WS row.
Next (dec) row (RS) Knit to last 3 sts, k2tog, k1—12 sts.
Cont in garter st and rep dec row every 8th row 3 times more, then every 4th row 6 times—3 sts. Work 3 rows even, end with a WS row. Bind off rem 3 sts, leaving a long tail.

Finishing
With RS facing, thread tail through sides of sts on shaped edge of flower. Pull to gather and spiral, forming flower shape. Secure end. Sew leaves to sides of flower, using photo as guide. Sew pin back to center of flower. ✤

Two Skeins

Pleated Cowl

Pleated Cowl

Bring an Elizabethan flair to modern times with this structured cowl, softened by carefully placed pleats.

Designed by Carolyn Noyes

Skill Level:

■■■□

Materials

- 2 1¾oz/50g skeins (each approx 198yd/181m) of Noro *Shiraito* (cashmere/angora/wool) in #31 mustard/green/purple/magenta ⓵
- One pair size 7 (4.5mm) needles OR SIZE TO OBTAIN GAUGE
- Size 7 (4.5mm) crochet hook
- Stitch markers
- Scrap yarn
- Embroidery needle and embroidery floss for lifeline

Size
Instructions are written for one size.

Knitted Measurements
Upper circumference 20"/51cm
Lower circumference 34"/86cm
Length 10"/25.5cm

Gauge
20 sts and 28 rows to 4"/10cm over St st using size 7 (4.5mm) needles. TAKE TIME TO CHECK GAUGE.

Stitch Glossary
Mp (make pleat) Wyif, insert needle from top in next st in marked row below; pick up this st, place on LH needle and purl tog with next st on current row. Remove floss.

Provisional Cast-On
With scrap yarn and crochet hook, ch the number of sts to cast on plus a few extra. Cut a tail and pull the tail through the last chain. With knitting needle and yarn, pick up and knit the stated number of sts through the "purl bumps" on the back of the chain. To remove scrap yarn chain, when instructed, pull out the tail from the last crochet stitch. Gently and slowly pull on the tail to unravel the crochet stitches, carefully placing each released knit stitch on a needle.

Short Row Sequence
Short row 1 Knit to 1 st before marker, sl the next st purlwise wyib. Move the yarn between the needles to front of work. Sl the same st back to left needle. Turn, bringing yarn to purl side between the needles; purl to end of row.
Row 2 Knit to just before the wrapped st. Insert the RH needle under the wrap, and knit it tog with the st on the needle, k to end of row.
Row 3 (WS) Purl.
Rep rows 1–3 for short row sequence.

Cowl
Using provisional cast-on, cast on 20 sts, place marker (pm), cast on 25 sts—45 sts.
*Work 4 rows in St st (k on RS, p on WS).
Begin short row sequence
Work short row sequence 4 times.
With *WS* facing and embroidery needle, thread floss through the first 13 sts to mark row for pleat. Turn to work next RS row.
Work short row sequence 3 times, then rep rows 1 and 2 of short row sequence.
Next (pleat) row (WS) MP in next 13 sts, p to end.

Rep short row sequence 4 times more. Work 9 rows in St st.
With *RS* facing and embroidery needle, thread floss through the
first 24 sts to mark row for pleat.
Work 8 rows in St st.
Next (pleat) row (WS) P to last 24 sts, MP to end of row.
Rep from * 3 times more.
Work 2 rows in St st.
Work short row sequence twice.

Finishing
Undo provisional cast-on and place sts on needle. Graft ends
together using Kitchener st.
I-cord edgings
With RS facing, pick up and k 96 sts along top edge. *Join yarn to
first st on LH needle and cast on 3 sts; k3, return sts to LH needle,
*k2, SKP; return 3 sts to LH needle; rep from * until all edge sts
have been worked and 3 sts rem. Knit 1 row, graft open sts to beg
of I-cord using Kitchener st.
With RS facing, pick up and k 188 sts along lower edge. Rep from *
as for top edge. ❖

Three Skeins

Twig Lace Shrug

Twig Lace Shrug

The delicate twig motif on the center back of this shrug is framed by columns of seed stitch.

Designed by Heather Boyd

Skill Level:

■■■□

Materials

- 3 (4, 4) 1¾oz/50g skeins (each approx 156yd/142m) of Noro *Ayatori* (wool/silk) in #15 sienna/turquoise/green/orange (2)
- One pair size 7 (4.5mm) needles OR SIZE TO OBTAIN GAUGE
- Size 6 (4mm) circular needle, 29"/80cm long
- Stitch markers

Sizes

Instructions are written for size Small. Changes for Medium and Large are in parentheses. (Shown in size Small.)

Knitted Measurements

Width 22 (24, 25)"/56 (61, 63.5)cm
Height 18 (20, 22)"/45.5 (51, 58.5)cm

Gauge

18 sts and 26 rows to 4"/10cm over St st using size 7 (4.5mm) needles. TAKE TIME TO CHECK GAUGE.

K1, P1 Rib

(over an even number of sts)
Row 1 (RS) *K1, p1; rep from * to end.
Row 2 K the knit sts and p the purl sts.
Rep row 2 for k1, p1 rib.

Twig Lace Pat

(worked over 32 sts)
Row 1 K9, k2tog, k1, yo, k1, yo, k1, ssk, k3, k2tog, k1, yo, k1, yo, k1, ssk, k6.
Row 2 and all WS rows Purl.
Row 3 K8, k2tog, k1, yo, k3, yo, k1, ssk, k1, k2tog, k1, yo, k3, yo, k1, ssk, k5.
Row 5 K7, k2tog, k1, yo, k5, yo, k1, sk2p, k1, yo, k5, yo, k1, ssk, k4.
Row 7 K6, k2tog, k1, yo, k1, yo, k1, ssk, k3, k2tog, k1, yo, k1, yo, k1, ssk, k9.
Row 9 K5, k2tog, k1, yo, k3, yo, k1, ssk, k1, k2tog, k1, yo, k3, yo, k1, ssk, k8.
Row 11 K4, k2tog, k1, yo, k5, yo, k1, sk2p, k1, yo, k5, yo, k1, ssk, k7.
Row 12 Purl.
Rep rows 1–12 for twig lace pat.

Note

Twig lace pat can be worked following chart *or* text. Chart can be found on page 137.

Shrug

With straight needles, cast on 100 (108, 112) sts loosely.
Row 1 (WS) Purl.
Row 2 (RS) K30 (34, 36), place marker (pm), [p1, k1] twice, pm, k32, pm, [p1, k1] twice, pm, k to end.
Row 3 P to first marker, sl marker (sm), [k1, p1] twice, sm, p to next marker, sm, [k1, p1] twice, sm, p to end.
Rep rows 2 and 3 once (once, twice) more.
Beg twig lace pat
Row 6 K to first marker, sm, [p1, k1] twice, sm, work row 1 of twig

lace pat over next 32 sts, sm, [p1, k1] twice, sm, k to end.

Row 7 P to first marker, sm, [k1, p1] twice, sm, work row 2 of twig lace pat over next 32 sts, sm, [k1, p1] twice, sm, p to end.

Cont in this manner until row 12 of twig lace pat is complete. Rep rows 1–12 of twig lace pat 8 (9, 10) times more. Piece should measure approx 17 (19, 21)"/43 (48, 53.5)cm from beg.

Next row (RS) K to first marker, sm, [p1, k1] twice, sm, k32, sm, [p1, k1] twice, sm, k to end.

Next row P to first marker, sm, [k1, p1] twice, sm, p to next marker, sm, [k1, p1] twice, sm, p to end.

Rep last 2 rows once (once, twice) more. Bind off loosely.

Finishing

Gently block piece to measurements.

Edging

With circular needle and RS facing, pick up and k 104 (112, 116) sts evenly along bound-off edge. Fold cast-on edge to bound-off edge to create armholes along sides and cont with working yarn, pick up and k 104 (112, 116) sts along cast-on edge—208 (224, 232) sts. Pm for beg of rnd. Work 16 rnds in k1, p1 rib. Bind off loosely in rib. ♣

One Skein

Lacy Collar

Lacy Collar

A soft-hued lace collar with ruffled edges is an accessory that's both sweetly retro and distinctly modern.

Designed by Wei Wilkins

Skill Level:
■■■□

Materials
- 1 3½oz/100g skein (each approx 462yd/422m) of Noro *Taiyo Sock* (cotton/wool/nylon/silk) in #8 teals/grey/khaki (1)
- Sizes 2, 3, and 4 (2.75, 3.25, and 3.5mm) circular needles, 24"/60cm long, OR SIZE TO OBTAIN GAUGE
- Size D/3 (3.25mm) crochet hook
- One ½"/15mm button

Size
Instructions are written for one size.

Knitted Measurements
Width approx 3"/7.5cm
Length approx 15½"/39.5cm

Gauge
27 sts and 38 rows to 4"/10cm over jadeite lace pat using size 2½ (3mm) needles. TAKE TIME TO CHECK GAUGE.

Stitch Glossary
sc Single crochet.

Jadeite Lace Pattern
Row 1 (RS) K1, ssk, *yo, k1, yo, ssk, yo, SK2P; rep from * across, ending last rep ssk, k1.
Rows 2, 4, 6, and 8 Purl.
Row 3 K2, *k3, yo, SK2P, yo; rep from * to last st, k1.
Row 5 K1, yo, *ssk, yo, Sk2P, yo, k1, yo; rep from * to last 2 sts, ssk.
Row 7 K2, *yo, SK2P, yo, k3; rep from * to last st, k1.
Rep rows 1–8 for jadeite lace pat.

Note
Piece is worked back and forth in rows. Circular needles are used to accommodate large number of sts; do not join.

Collar
With size 3 (3.25mm) needle, cast on 105 sts. Change to size 2 (2.75mm) needle and work 3 rows in garter st.
Begin jadeite lace pat
Work rows 1–8 of jadeite lace pat 3 times, working each rep with the next larger size needle. Bind off loosely.

Finishing
Edging
Place markers ¾"/2cm down from upper edge on each side of collar. With RS facing and size 4 (3.5mm) needle, beg along left side edge of piece, pick up and k 6 sts along side edge to marker, *yo, pick up and k 2 sts; rep from * to next marker, pick up and k 5 sts—200 sts.
Row 1 (buttonhole) P2, bind off 2 sts, purl to end.
Row 2 K5, *k2tog, yo; rep from * to last 3 sts, k1, yo for buttonhole, k2.
Row 3 P2, [k1, p1] in yo, purl to end (inc one additional st in the middle of the row)—201 sts.
Row 4 K6, *yo, ssk; rep from * to last 5 sts, k5.
Next row Bind off 5 sts; with crochet hook, *ch 2, sc in next st; rep from * to last 5 sts, bind off to end.
Sew button opposite buttonhole. ❧

Two Skeins

Swiss Scarf

Swiss Scarf

Luxury meets whimsy in a funky geometric scarf worked in rich jewel tones.

Designed by Jacqueline Jewett

Skill Level:
■■■□

Materials

- 2 1¾oz/50g skeins (each approx 110yd/100m) of Noro *Kureyon* (wool) in #188 olive/lilac/purple/grey (4)
- One pair each sizes 6 and 8 (4 and 5mm) needles OR SIZE TO OBTAIN GAUGE

Size

Instructions are written for one size.

Knitted Measurements

Width 6"/15cm
Length 48"/122cm

Gauge

18 sts and 24 rows to 4"/10cm in St st using size 8 (5mm) needles.
TAKE TIME TO CHECK GAUGE.

Stitch Glossary

kfb Knit into the front and back of st—1 st increased.
M1 p-st Insert needle from front to back under the strand between the last st worked and the next st on the LH needle. Purl into the back loop to twist the st.

Scarf

Lower border

With smaller needles, cast on 24 sts. Work in St st (k on RS, p on WS) for 8 rows. Change to larger needles.
Next row (RS) Cast on 2 sts, k to end.
Next row Cast on 2 sts, p to last 2 sts, k2—28 sts.
Keeping first 2 and last 2 sts in garter st, work 6 rows more in St st.

Begin main pat

Row 1 (RS) K4, k2tog, turn.
Row 2 (WS) P3, k2.
Row 3 K5, turn.
Rows 4–8 Rep rows 2 and 3 twice more, then row 2 once.
Row 9 (RS) K4, kfb, [yo] 4 times, ssk, k4, k2tog, turn.
Row 10 P5, p2tog (working yo tog with st), turn.
Row 11 K6.
Rows 12–16 Rep rows 10 and 11 twice more, then row 10 once.
Row 17 K5, kfb, [yo] 4 times, ssk, k4, k2tog, turn.
Rows 18–24 Rep rows 10–16.
Row 19 (RS) K5, kfb, [yo] 4 times, ssk, k4, turn.
Row 20 K2, p1, p2tog (working yo tog with st), turn.
Row 21 K5.
Rows 22–25 Rep rows 20 and 21 twice more, then row 20 once.
Row 26 (WS) K2, p3, M1 p-st, turn.
Row 27 K6.
Row 28 (WS) K2, p24, k2.
Row 29 Knit.
Rows 30–32 Rep rows 28 and 29 twice more.
Row 33 (RS) K8, k2tog, turn.
Row 34 P7, k2.
Row 35 K9.
Rows 36–40 Rep rows 34 and 35 twice more, then row 34 once more.
Row 41 K8, kfb, [yo] 4 times, ssk, k4, k2tog, turn.
Row 42 P6, turn.
Row 43 K6, turn.
Rows 44–47 Rep rows 42 and 43 twice more.
Row 48 P6, M1 p-st, turn.
Row 49 K6, kfb, [yo] 4 times, ssk, k8, turn.
Row 50 K2, p7, turn.
Row 51 K9, turn.
Rows 52–55 Rep rows 50 and 51 twice more.
Row 56 K2, p7, M1 p-st, turn.
Row 57 K10, turn.
Rows 58–62 Rep rows 28–32.
Rep rows 1–62 seven times more, then rows 1–32 once.

Upper border

Next row (RS) Bind off 2 sts, k to end.
Next row Bind off 2 sts, p to end.
Change to smaller needles. Work 8 rows in St st. Bind off. ❧

One Skein

Head Kerchief

Head Kerchief

Turn a bad hair day into a high-style moment with this striking lacy kerchief.

Designed by Lauren Waterfield

Skill Level:
■■■□

Materials
■ 1 1¾oz/50g skein (each approx 137yd/125m) of Noro *Silk Garden Lite* (silk/kid mohair/lambswool) in #2080 green/purple/orange/rose **(3)**
■ One pair size 6 (4mm) needles OR SIZE TO OBTAIN GAUGE
■ Size G/6 (4mm) crochet hook

Size
Instructions are written for one size.

Knitted Measurements
Width (excluding ties) approx 20"/51cm
Length approx 11"/28cm

Gauge
17 sts and 26 rows to 4"/10cm over pat st using size 6 (4mm) needles. TAKE TIME TO CHECK GAUGE.

Lace Pattern
(multiple of 8 sts)
Row 1 (RS) Knit.
Row 2 and all WS rows Purl.
Row 3 *K6, k2tog, yo; rep from * to end.
Row 5 *Yo, ssk, k3, k2tog, yo, k1; rep from * to end.
Row 7 *Ssk, k6, yo; rep from * to end.
Row 9 Knit.
Row 11 *K2, k2tog, yo, k4; rep from * to end.
Row 13 *K1, k2tog, yo, k1, yo, ssk, k2; rep from * to end.
Row 15 *K3, yo, ssk, k3; rep from * to end.
Row 16 Purl.
Rep rows 1–16 for lace pat.

Note
When working lace pat, if there are not enough sts to work both a yarn over and the compensating decrease, work sts in St st.

Kerchief
Cast on 2 sts.
Set-up row (WS) [Kfb] twice—4 sts.
Row 1 (RS) Kfb, k2, kfb—6 sts.
Row 2 and all WS rows K2, purl to last 2 sts, k2.
Row 3 K2, yo, k2, yo, k2—8 sts.
Row 5 K2, yo, k2tog, yo, k2, yo, k2—10 sts.
Row 7 K2, yo, k2tog, yo, k1, yo, ssk, k1, yo, k2—12 sts.
Row 9 K2, yo, work row 15 of lace pat over next 8 sts, yo, k2—14 sts.
Row 11 K2, yo, k1, work row 1 of lace pat over next 8 sts, k1, yo, k2—16 sts.
Row 13 K2, yo, k2tog, yo, work row 3 of lace pat over next 8 sts, k2, yo, k2—18 sts.
Cont in this manner, inc 2 sts each row, working inc'd sts into lace pat until there are 78 sts, end with a RS row. Knit 2 rows. Bind off knitwise.

Finishing
Ties (make 2)
With crochet hook, make a chain approx 5"/12.5cm long. Attach one tie to each top corner of bound-off row. ❖

Three Skeins

Daisy Stitch Capelet

Daisy Stitch Capelet

A delicate daisy stitch pattern beautifully complements a soft and feminine colorway of *Koromo*.

Designed by Dorcas Lavery

Skill Level:

■■□□

Materials

- 3 1¾oz/50g skeins (each approx 137yd/126m) of Noro *Koromo* (cotton/wool/silk) in #2 mauve/lilac/violet/purple/limoncello (4)
- One each sizes 8 and 10 (5 and 6mm) circular needle, 29"/80cm long, OR SIZE TO OBTAIN GAUGE
- Stitch marker
- One button, 1¼"/32mm diameter

Size

Instructions are written for one size.

Knitted Measurements

Circumference at hem 44½"/113cm
Length 12½"/32cm

Gauge

16 sts and 25 rows to 4"/10cm over daisy st using size 10 (6mm) needles. TAKE TIME TO CHECK GAUGE.

Seed Stitch

(over an even number of sts)
Row 1 (RS) *K1, p1; rep from * to end.
Row 2 K the purl sts and p the knit sts.
Rep row 2 for seed st.

Daisy Stitch

(multiple of 10 sts)
Rows 1 and 3 (RS) Knit.
Rows 2 and 4 Purl.
Row 5 *Insert RH needle into the st 3 rows below the 3rd st on LH needle, draw through a loop and place on RH needle, k2, draw a 2nd loop through the same st 3 rows below and place on RH needle, k3, draw a 3rd loop through the same st 3 rows below and place on RH needle, k5; rep from * to end.
Row 6 *[P5, p2tog tbl (loop and next st), p1] twice, p2tog tbl (loop and next st); rep from * to end.
Rows 7 and 9 Knit.
Rows 8 and 10 Purl.
Row 11 *K5, insert RH needle into st 3 rows below 3rd st on LH needle, draw through a loop and place on RH needle, k2, draw a 2nd loop through the same st 3 rows below and place on RH needle, k3, draw a 3rd loop through the same st 3 rows below and place on RH needle; rep from * to end.
Row 12 *[P2tog tbl (loop and next st), p1] twice, purl together loop and next st tbl, p5; rep from * to end.
Rep rows 1–12 for daisy st.

Note

Circular needles are used to accommodate the large number of stitches. Do not join.

Capelet

With larger needle, cast on 178 sts. Do not join. Work 4 rows in seed st.
Row 1 (RS) Work 4 sts in seed st, work 10-st rep of daisy st 17 times, work 4 sts in seed st.

Row 2 Work 4 sts in seed st, work 10-st rep of daisy st 17 times, work 4 sts in seed st.

Cont in this manner, working first and last 4 sts in seed st, until row 12 of daisy st is complete. Rep rows 1–12 four times more.

Next (dec) row (RS) Work 4 sts in seed st, *ssk, k1, k2tog, k5; rep from * to last 4 sts, work 4 sts in seed st—144 sts.

Next (dec) row (WS) Work 4 sts in seed st, SK2P, k1, p1, *SK2P, [p1, k1] twice, p1; rep from * to last 7 sts, SK2P, work 4 sts in seed st—108 sts. Change to smaller needle.

Row 1 (RS) K1, p1, k1, p2, *k1, p1; rep from * to last 5 sts, k2, p1, k1, p1.

Row 2 K1, p1, k1, p2, *k1, p1; rep from * to last 5 sts, k2, p1, k1, p1.

Row 3 (buttonhole row) K1, bind off 2 sts, work in pat to end of row.

Row 4 Work in pat to end of row, casting on 2 sts over bound-off sts.

Rows 5 and 7 K1, p1, k1, p2, *k1, p1; rep from * to last 5 sts, k2, p1, k1, p1.

Rows 6 and 8 K1, p1, k1, p2, *k1, p1; rep from * to last 5 sts, k2, p1, k1, p1.

Bind off in pat.

Finishing

Sew button to right front edge opposite buttonhole. ✤

Three Skeins

Braided Moebius Cowl

Braided Moebius Cowl

A braid of strips knit in three different color-ways can be worn long or doubled for extra warmth.

Designed by Linda Voss Plummer

Skill Level:

■■■□

Materials

- 1 1¾oz/50g skein (each approx 137yd/125m) of Noro *Shiro* (wool/cashmere/silk) each in #1 black/tan/green (A), #2 grey/sand/turquoise (B), and #6 turquoise/blue/pink/brown (C) **③**
- One pair size 7 (4.5mm) needles OR SIZE TO OBTAIN GAUGE
- Size 7 (4.5mm) crochet hook
- Scrap yarn
- Stitch holders

Size

Instructions are written for one size.

Knitted Measurements

Length approx 38"/96.5cm
Width approx 3½"/9cm

Gauge

36 sts and 26 rows to 4"/10cm over rib pat using size 7 (4.5mm) needles, unstretched. TAKE TIME TO CHECK GAUGE.

Provisional Cast-On

With crochet hook and scrap yarn, ch number of sts indicated plus a few extra. Cut a tail and pull the tail through last chain. With knitting needle and yarn, pick up and knit the stated number of sts through the bumps on the back of the chain. To remove scrap yarn, when instructed, pull out the tail from the last crochet st. Gently and slowly pull on the tail to unravel the crochet sts, carefully placing each released knit stitch on a needle.

Rib Pattern

(multiple of 5 sts plus 3)
Row 1 (RS) *K3, p2; rep from * across, end k3.
Row 2 *P3, k2; rep from * across, end p3.
Rep rows 1 and 2 for rib pat.

Cowl

Strip (make 3)

Cast on 18 sts using provisional cast-on. With A, work in rib pat until approx 24"/61cm of yarn rem. Place sts on holder.
Rep with B and C.

Finishing

Place strips side by side on a flat surface with cast-on edges at top. Beg at top and, keeping pieces flat, braid strips tog. When braid is complete, tack pieces tog at end. (Unravel strips, if necessary, until they are all the same length.) Holding both ends of braid, carefully give the piece a half twist to form moebius. Place sts of A strip from holder on needle. Carefully remove scrap yarn from A strip and place sts on a 2nd needle. Graft ends tog using Kitchener st. Rep for B and C strips. ✤

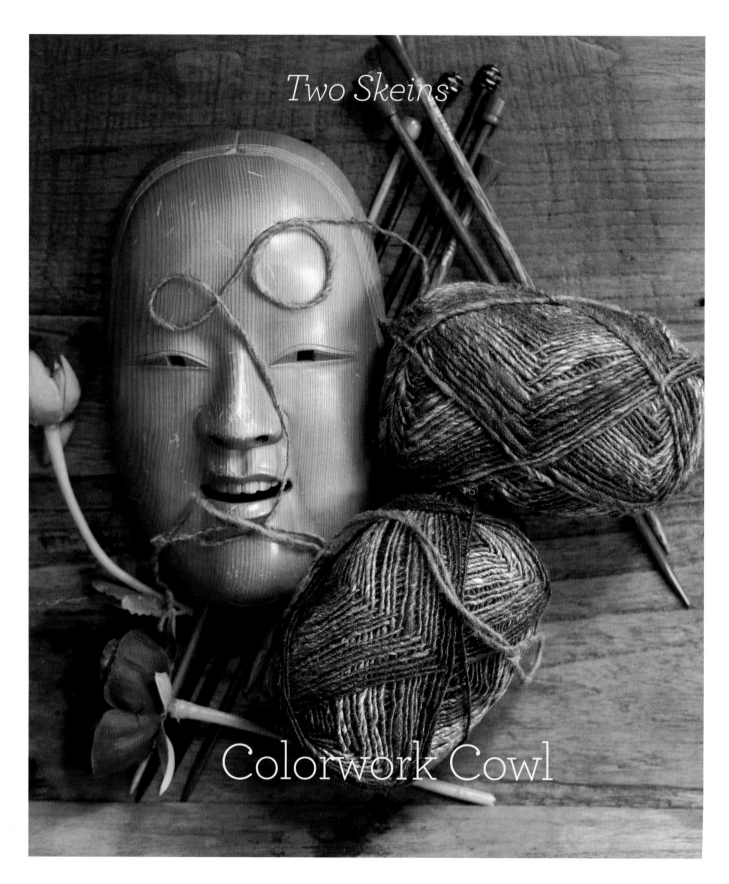

Two Skeins

Colorwork Cowl

Colorwork Cowl

Luxe buttons bring out the rich tones in this uniquely patterned cowl knit in a tube.

Designed by Barb Brown

Skill Level:

■■■□

Materials

- 1 1¾oz/50g skein (each approx 148yd/135m) of Noro *Takeuma* (wool/silk/viscose) in #7 neutrals (CC) **(4)**
- One set (5) size 6 (4mm) double-pointed needles (dpns) OR SIZE TO OBTAIN GAUGE
- Stitch marker
- 3 buttons, approx ⅝"/15mm diameter
- Crochet hook and scrap yarn for provisional cast-on

Size

Instructions are written for one size.

Knitted Measurements

Width 3"/7.5cm
Length approx 44"/112cm

Gauge

22 sts and 20 rnds to 4"/10cm over pat st using size 6 (4mm) needles.
TAKE TIME TO CHECK GAUGE.

Color Pattern I

(multiple of 10 sts)
Rnd 1 *With MC, k1; with CC, k1; [with MC, k1; with CC, k2] twice, with MC, k1; with CC, k1; rep from * to end of rnd.
Rep rnd 1 for color pat I.

Color Pattern II

(multiple of 10 sts)
Rnd 1 *With CC, k1; with MC, k1; [with CC, k1; with MC, k2] twice, with CC, k1; with MC, k1; rep from * to end of rnd.
Rep rnd 1 for color pat II.

Stripe Sequence

*Work 9 rnds color pat I, 9 rnds color pat II, 3 rnds pat I, 5 rnds pat II, 5 rnds pat I, 3 rnds pat II**, 7 rnds pat I, 9 rnds pat II, 3 rnds pat I, 7 rnds pat II, 9 rnds pat I, 3 rnds pat II***.

Provisional Cast-On

With scrap yarn and crochet hook, ch the number of sts to cast on plus a few extra. Cut a tail and pull the tail through the last chain. With knitting needle and yarn, pick up and knit the stated number of sts through the "purl bumps" on the back of the chain. To remove scrap yarn chain, when instructed, pull out the tail from the last crochet stitch. Gently and slowly pull on the tail to unravel the crochet stitches, carefully placing each released knit stitch on a needle.

Note

If the colors line up with insufficient contrast, break one yarn and remove that section. Set aside to use in finishing the scarf.

Cowl

Using provisional cast-on, with MC, cast on 40 sts and divide evenly on 4 dpns. Place marker (pm) for beg of rnd and join, being careful not to twist sts. Knit 1 rnd.
Work in stripe sequence from * to *** twice, then from * to ** once.
Next rnd With MC, k20 and place sts on 1st needle (N1), k20 and place sts on 2nd needle (N2).

Button band
Next (joining) row With one strand each of MC and CC held tog, knit first st of each needle tog, *knit next st of each needle tog; rep from * to end—20 sts.

Cont with both strands held tog, knit 8 rows. Bind off knitwise.

Buttonhole band
Carefully undo provisional cast-on and place first 20 sts on N1 and last 20 sts on N2.

Next row Join as for button band.

Cont with both strands held tog, knit 3 rows.

Next (buttonhole) row K3, yo, k2tog, k4, yo, k2tog, k4, k2tog, yo, k3. Work 4 rows more in garter st. Bind off knitwise.

Finishing
Sew buttons to RS of button band, opposite buttonholes. ♣

Two Skeins

Bunny Toy

Bunny Toy

This adorable plush bunny is knit in playful stripes drawn from different sections of the same colorway.

Designed by Carol J. Sulcoski

Skill Level:

■■■□

Materials

■ 2 3½oz/100g skeins (each approx 142yd/130m) of Noro *Nadeshiko* (angora/wool/silk) in #18 beige/taupe/jade/hot pink (5)
■ One set (5) size 9 (5.5mm) double-pointed needles (dpns) OR SIZE TO OBTAIN GAUGE
■ Stitch marker
■ Scrap yarn and embroidery needle for eyes, nose, and whiskers
■ Polyester stuffing

Knitted Measurements

Height 10"/25.5cm

Gauge

12 sts and 20 rows to 4"/10cm over St st using size 9 (5.5mm) needles. TAKE TIME TO CHECK GAUGE.

Stitch Glossary

Kfb Knit into the front and back of st—1 st increased.

Notes

1) Body is knit in the round from the bottom up.
2) Ears are knit separately and sewn on.
3) For CC stripes, use the 2nd skein of yarn, starting with a different color run.

Bunny

Body

Cast on 4 sts. Place marker (pm) for beg of rnd and join, being careful not to twist sts.

Rnd 1 *Kfb, k1; rep from * to end—6 sts.
Rnd 2 *Kfb, k2; rep from * to end—8 sts.
Rnd 3 *Kfb, k1; rep from * to end—12 sts.
Rnd 4 Rep rnd 3—18 sts.
Rnd 5 Knit.
Rnd 6 *K2, kfb; rep from * to end—24 sts.
Rnd 7 Knit.
Rnd 8 *K3, kfb; rep from * to end—30 sts.
Rnd 9 Knit.
Rnd 10 *K4, kfb; rep from * to end—36 sts.
Rnd 11 Knit.
Rnd 12 *K5, kfb; rep from * to end—42 sts.
Rnd 13 Knit.
Rnd 14 *K6, kfb; rep from * to end—48 sts.
Rnd 15 Knit.

Begin stripe pattern

With CC, knit 2 rnds.
With MC, knit 2 rnds.
With CC, knit 2 rnds.
With MC, knit 1 rnd.
Next (inc) rnd With MC, *k7, kfb; rep from * to end—54 sts.
With CC, knit 2 rnds.
With MC, knit 2 rnds.
With CC, knit 1 rnd.
Next (inc) rnd With CC, *k8, kfb; rep from * to end—60 sts.
With MC, knit 2 rnds.

Neck and head shaping

With CC, knit 1 rnd.

Next (dec) rnd With CC, *k4, k2tog; rep from * to end—50 sts.
With MC, knit 2 rnds.
With CC, knit 1 rnd.
Next (dec) rnd With CC, *k3, k2tog; rep from * to end—40 sts.
With MC, knit 2 rnds.
With CC, knit 1 rnd.
Next (dec) rnd With CC, *k2, k2tog; rep from * to end—30 sts.
Place marker in last rnd. Break CC.
With MC, work even until head measures 2½"/6.5cm from marker.
Next rnd *K5, ssk, k1, k2tog, k5; rep from * to end—26 sts.
Next rnd *K4, ssk, k1, k2tog, k4; rep from * to end—22 sts.
Next rnd K5, then bind off all sts. Break yarn, leaving an 18"/46cm tail.

Ears (make 2)

With CC, cast on 10 sts. Pm and join, being careful not to twist sts.
With CC, knit 3 rnds.
With MC, knit 1 rnd.
Rep these 4 rnds 2 times more.
With CC, knit 3 rnds.
Next rnd With MC, *ssk, k1, k2tog; rep from * to end—6 sts.
With CC, knit 1 rnd.
Next rnd With CC, *sk2p; rep from * to end—2 sts.
Break yarn, leaving a 12"/30cm tail. Draw tail through rem sts, pull tight and secure.

Finishing

Make a loose pompom and sew in place on lower body for tail. Stuff body and head with polyester stuffing and sew top of head closed. With scrap yarn and embroidery needle, embroider eyes, nose, and whiskers using photo as guide. Sew ears in place on head. ❖

Honeycomb Cable Hat
(Continued from page 13)

Stitch Key

☐	K on RS, p on WS
−	P on RS, k on WS
O	Yo
⟋	K2tog
⟍	Ssk
3-st RC
3-st LC
4-st RC
(shaded)	No stitch

CHART 1

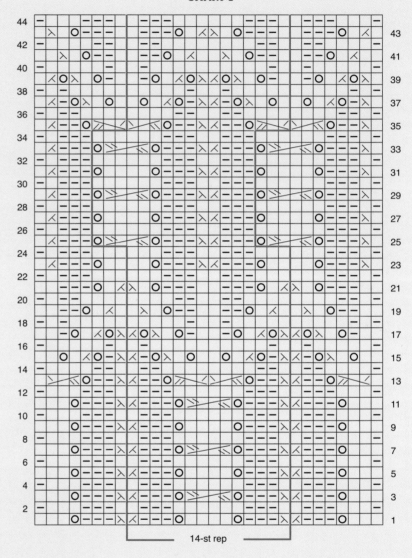

14-st rep

CHART 2

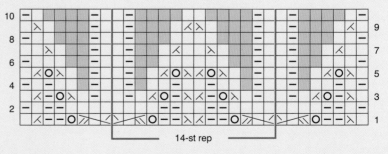

14-st rep

Twisted-Stitch Mitts
(Continued from page 25)

CHART 1

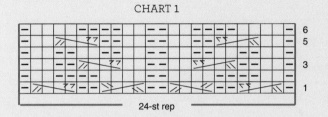

24-st rep

Stitch Key

☐	Knit
⊟	Purl
⧄	2-st RC
⧄	2-st RPC
⧄	2-st LPC
⧄	3-st LC
⧄	4-st RC
⧄	4-st LC
⧄	4-st RPC
⧄	4-st LPC

CHART 2

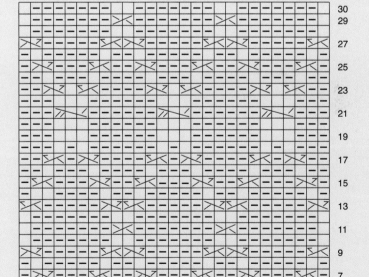

27 sts

Lace Cardi
(Continued from page 29)

Stitch Key

☐ K on RS, p on WS

Ⓞ Yo

◩ K2tog

◪ Ssk

⊠ SKP

▨ No stitch

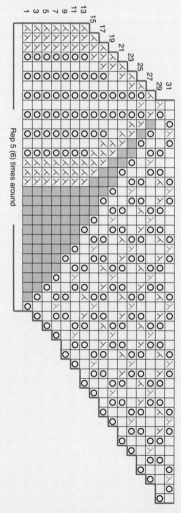

CHART 2

Rep 5 (6) times around

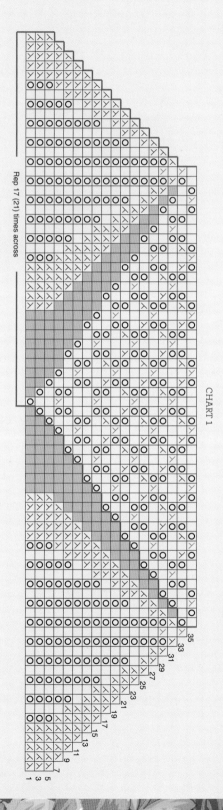

CHART 1

Rep 17 (21) times across

Cabled Handbag
(Continued from page 33)

Stitch Key

☐	Knit
⊟	Purl
	4-st RPC
	4-st LPC
	6-st RC
	6-st LC

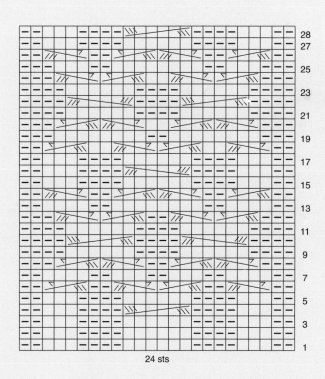

Stitch Key

☐ K on RS, p on WS

⊙ Yo

⋏ S2KP

Collared Lace Shawl
(Continued from page 37)

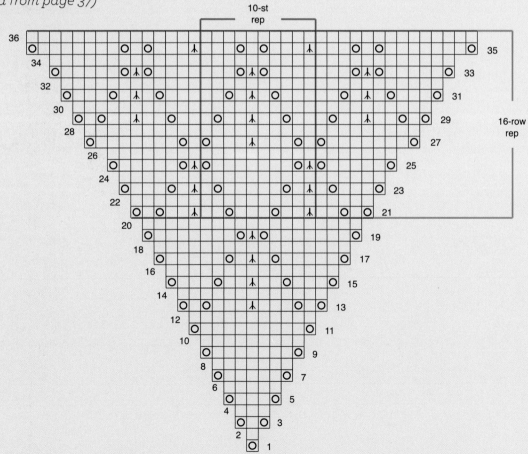

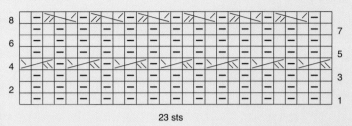

8

6

4

2

7

5

3

1

23 sts

Stitch Key

☐ K on RS, p on WS

⊟ P on RS, k on WS

▨ 3-st RC

▨ 3-st LC

Lattice Cable Mitts
(*Continued from page 57*)

VERTICAL
EYELET CHART

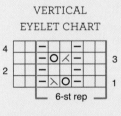

4

2

3

1

6-st rep

HORIZONTAL
EYELET CHART

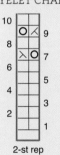

10

9

8

7

6

5

4

3

2

1

2-st rep

Stitch Key

☐ K on RS, p on WS

⊟ P on RS, k on WS

⊙ Yo

◩ K2tog

◪ Ssk

Eyelet Lace Shawlette
(*Continued from page 77*)

CHART 2

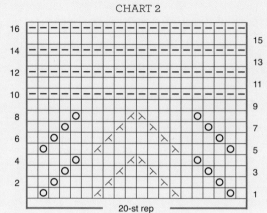

20-st rep

Chevron Cape
(Continued from page 89)

CHART 1

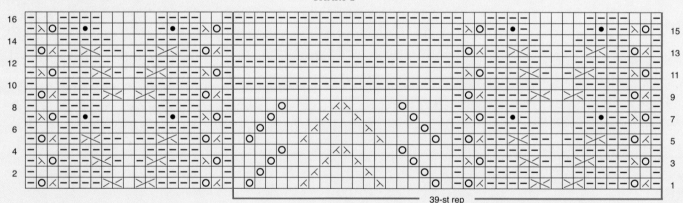

39-st rep

Stitch Key

- ☐ K on RS, p on WS
- ⊟ P on RS, k on WS
- ◯ Yo
- ◿ K2tog
- ◺ Ssk
- ⧖ RT
- ⧖ LT
- ● Make bobble

Stitch Key

☐ K on RS, p on WS

◙ Yo

⟋ K2tog

⟍ Ssk

⟑ S2KP

Twig Lace Shrug

(Continued from page 101)

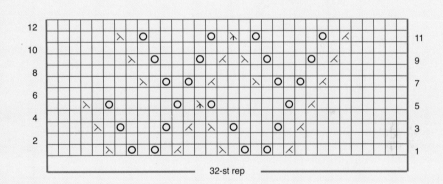

32-st rep

Helpful Information

Abbreviations

approx	approximately	pm	place marker
beg	begin(ning)	psso	pass slip stitch(es) over
CC	contrasting color	rem	remain(s)(ing)
ch	chain	rep	repeat(s)(ing)(ed)
cm	centimeter(s)	RH	right-hand
cn	cable needle	rnd(s)	round(s)
cont	continu(e)(ing)	RS	right side(s)
dec	decreas(e)(ing)	S2KP	slip 2 stitches together knitwise, knit 1, pass 2 slip stitches over knit 1
dpn(s)	double-pointed needle(s)		
est	establish(ed)(ing)	SK2P	slip 1 knitwise, knit 2 together, pass slip stitch over the knit 2 together
foll	follow(s)(ing)		
g	gram(s)	SKP	slip 1 knitwise, knit 1, pass slip stitch over
inc	increas(e)(ing)	sl	slip
k	knit	sl st	slip stitch
k2tog	knit 2 stitches together	sm	slip marker
kfb	knit into front and back of stitch	ssk	slip, slip, knit (see glossary)
LH	left-hand	ssp	slip the next 2 sts one at a time purlwise to RH needle, insert tip of LH needle into fronts of these sts and purl them together
lp(s)	loop(s)		
m	meter(s)		
MB	make bobble	sssk	see glossary
MC	main color	st(s)	stitch(es)
mm	millimeter(s)	St st	stockinette stitch
M1	make one (see glossary)	tbl	through back loop(s)
M1-P	make 1 purl stitch (see glossary)	tog	together
oz	ounce(s)	w&t	wrap and turn
p	purl	WS	wrong side(s)
p2tog	purl 2 stitches together	wyib	with yarn in back
pat(s)	pattern(s)	wyif	with yarn in front
		yd	yard(s)
		yo	yarn over needle
		*	repeat directions following * as many times as indicated
		[ ]	repeat directions inside brackets as many times as indicated

Checking Your Gauge

Make a test swatch at least 4"/10cm square. If the number of stitches and rows does not correspond to the gauge given, you must change the needle size. An easy rule to follow is: To get fewer stitches to the inch/cm, use a larger needle; to get more stitches to the inch/cm, use a smaller needle. Continue to try different needle sizes until you get the same number of stitches in the gauge.

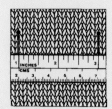

Stitches measured over 2"/5cm

Rows measured over 2"/5cm

Skill Levels

■□□□
Beginner
Ideal first project.

■■□□
Easy
Basic stitches, minimal shaping and simple finishing.

■■■□
Intermediate
For knitters with some experience. More intricate stitches, shaping and finishing.

■■■■
Experienced
For knitters able to work patterns with complicated shaping and finishing.

Knitting Needle Sizes

U.S.	Metric	U.S.	Metric
0	2mm	10	6mm
1	2.25mm	10½	6.5mm
2	2.75mm	11	8mm
3	3.25mm	13	9mm
4	3.5mm	15	10mm
5	3.75mm	17	12.75mm
6	4mm	19	15mm
7	4.5mm	35	19mm
8	5mm		
9	5.5mm		

Standard Yarn Weight System

Categories of yarn, gauge ranges, and recommended needle and hook sizes

Yarn Weight Symbol & Category Names	0 Lace	1 Super Fine	2 Fine	3 Light	4 Medium	5 Bulky	6 Super Bulky
Type of Yarns in Category	Fingering 10 count crochet thread	Sock, Fingering, Baby	Sport, Baby	DK, Light Worsted	Worsted, Afghan, Aran	Chunky, Craft, Rug	Bulky, Roving
Knit Gauge Range* in Stockinette Stitch to 4 inches	33–40** sts	27–32 sts	23–26 sts	21–24 sts	16–20 sts	12–15 sts	6–11 sts
Recommended Needle in Metric Size Range	1.5–2.25 mm	2.25–3.25 mm	3.25–3.75 mm	3.75–4.5 mm	4.5–5.5 mm	5.5–8 mm	8 mm and larger
Recommended Needle U.S. Size Range	000 to 1	1 to 3	3 to 5	5 to 7	7 to 9	9 to 11	11 and larger
Crochet Gauge* Ranges in Single Crochet to 4 inch	32-42 double crochets**	21–32 sts	16–20 sts	12–17 sts	11–14 sts	8–11 sts	5–9 sts
Recommended Hook in Metric Size Range	Steel*** 1.6–1.4mm Regular hook 2.25 mm	2.25–3.5 mm	3.5–4.5 mm	4.5–5.5 mm	5.5–6.5 mm	6.5–9 mm	9 mm and larger
Recommended Hook U.S. Size Range	Steel*** 6, 7, 8 Regular hook B-1	B-1 to E-4	E-4 to 7	7 to I-9	I-9 to K-10½	K-10½ to M-13	M-13 and larger

*GUIDELINES ONLY: The above reflect the most commonly used gauges and needle or hook sizes for specific yarn categories.

**Lace weight yarns are usually knitted or crocheted on larger needles and hooks to create lacy, openwork patterns. Accordingly, a gauge range is difficult to determine. Always follow the gauge stated in your pattern.

*** Steel crochet hooks are sized differently from regular hooks-the higher the number, the smaller the hook, which is the reverse of regular hook sizing.

This Standards & Guidelines booklet and downloadable symbol artwork are available at YarnStandards.com.

Glossary

as foll Work the instructions that follow.

bind off Used to finish an edge or segment. Lift the first stitch over the second, the second over the third, etc. (U.K.: cast off)

bind off in ribbing Work in ribbing as you bind off. (Knit the knit stitches, purl the purl stitches.) (U.K.: cast off in ribbing)

3-needle bind-off With the right side of the two pieces facing and the needles parallel, insert a third needle into the first stitch on each needle and knit them together. Knit the next two stitches the same way. Slip the first stitch on the third needle over the second stitch and off the needle. Repeat for three-needle bind-off.

cast on Placing a foundation row of stitches upon the needle in order to begin knitting.

decrease Reduce the stitches in a row (that is, knit 2 together).

hold to front (back) of work Usually refers to stitches placed on a cable needle that are held to the front (or back) of the work as it faces you.

increase Add stitches in a row (that is, knit in front and back of stitch).

knitwise Insert the needle into the stitch as if you were going to knit it.

make one With the needle tip, lift the strand between the last stitch knit and the next stitch on the left-hand needle and knit into back of it. One knit stitch has been added.

make one p-st With the needle tip, lift the strand between the last stitch worked and the next stitch on the left-hand needle and purl it. One purl stitch has been added.

no stitch On some charts, "no stitch" is indicated with shaded spaces where stitches have been decreased or not yet made. In such cases, work the stitches of the chart, skipping over the "no stitch" spaces.

place markers Place or attach a loop of contrast yarn or purchased stitch marker as indicated.

pick up and knit (purl) Knit (or purl) into the loops along an edge.

purlwise Insert the needle into the stitch as if you were going to purl it.

selvedge stitch Edge stitch that helps make seaming easier.

slip, slip, knit Slip next two stitches knitwise, one at a time, to right-hand needle. Insert tip of left-hand needle into fronts of these stitches, from left to right. Knit them together. One stitch has been decreased.

slip, slip, slip, knit Slip next three stitches knitwise, one at a time, to right-hand needle. Insert tip of left-hand needle into fronts of these stitches, from left to right. Knit them together. Two stitches have been decreased.

slip stitch An unworked stitch made by passing a stitch from the left-hand to the right-hand needle as if to purl.

stockinette stitch Knit every right-side row and purl every wrong-side row.

work even Continue in pattern without increasing or decreasing. (U.K.: work straight)

work to end Work the established pattern to the end of the row.

yarn over Making a new stitch by wrapping the yarn over the right-hand needle. (U.K.: yfwd, yon, yrn)

Knitting Techniques

Kitchener Stitch (Grafting)

1. Insert tapestry needle purlwise (as shown) through first stitch on front needle. Pull yarn through, leaving that stitch on knitting needle.

2. Insert tapestry needle knitwise (as shown) through first stitch on back needle. Pull yarn through, leaving stitch on knitting needle.

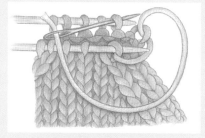

3. Insert tapestry needle knitwise through first stitch on front needle, slip stitch off needle and insert tapestry needle purlwise (as shown) through next stitch on front needle. Pull yarn through, leaving this stitch on needle.

4. Insert tapestry needle purlwise through first stitch on back needle. Slip stitch off needle and insert tapestry needle knitwise (as shown) through next stitch on back needle. Pull yarn through, leaving this stitch on needle.

Repeat steps 3 and 4 until all stitches on both front and back needles have been grafted. Fasten off and weave in end.

3-Needle Bind-Off

1. With the right side of the two pieces facing each other, and the needles parallel, insert a third needle knitwise into the first stitch of each needle. Wrap the yarn around the needle as if to knit.

2. Knit these two stitches together and slip them off the needles. *Knit the next two stitches together in the same way as shown.

3. Slip the first stitch on the third needle over the second stitch and off the needle. Repeat from the * in step 2 across the row until all the stitches are bound off.

Picking Up Stitches

Along a Horizontal Edge
1. Insert the knitting needle into the center of the first stitch in the row below the bound-off edge. Wrap the yarn knitwise around the needle.

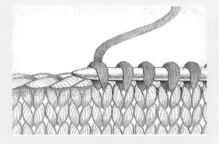

2. Draw the yarn through. You have picked up one stitch. Continue to pick up one stitch in each stitch along the bound-off edge.

Along a Vertical Edge
1. Insert the knitting needle into the corner stitch of the first row, one stitch in from the side edge. Wrap the yarn around the needle knitwise.

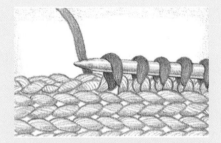

2. Draw the yarn through. You have picked up one stitch. Continue to pick up stitches along the edge. Occasionally skip one row to keep the edge from flaring.

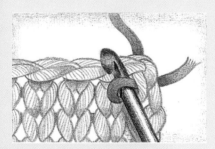

With a Crochet Hook
1. Insert the crochet hook from front to back into the center of the first stitch one row below the bound-off edge. Catch the yarn and pull a loop through.

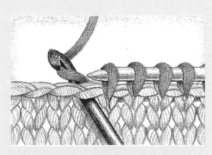

2. Slip the loop onto the knitting needle, being sure it is not twisted. Continue to pick up one stitch in each stitch along the bound-off edge.

Crocheted Chain

1. Make a slipknot and place it on the hook. Draw the yarn through the loop on the hook by catching it with the hook and pulling it toward you.

2. One chain stitch is complete. Lightly tug on the yarn to tighten the loop if it is very loose, or wiggle the hook to loosen the loop if it is tight. Repeat from step 1 to make as many chain stitches as required for your pattern.

Distributors

To locate retailers of Noro yarns, please contact one of the following distributors:

UK & EUROPE
Designer Yarns Ltd.
Units 8–10
Newbridge Industrial Estate
Pitt Street
Keighley BD21 4PQ
UNITED KINGDOM
Tel: +44 (0)1535 664222
Fax: +44 (0)1535 664333
Email: alex@designeryarns.uk.com
www.designeryarns.uk.com

USA
Knitting Fever Inc.
315 Bayview Avenue
Amityville, New York 11701
Tel: 001 516 546 3600
Fax: 001 516 546 6871
www.knittingfever.com

CANADA
Diamond Yarn Ltd.
155 Martin Ross Avenue
Unit 3
Toronto, Ontario M3J 2L9
Tel: 001 416 736 6111
Fax: 001 416 736 6112
www.diamondyarn.com

DENMARK
Fancy Knit
Hovedvjen 71
8586 Oerum Djurs Ramten
Tel: +45 59 4621 89
Email: roenneburg@mail.dk

**GERMANY / AUSTRIA /
SWITZERLAND/
BELGIUM / NETHERLANDS/
LUXEMBOURG**
Designer Yarns (Deutschland) GMBH
Welserstrasse 10g
D-51149 Koln
GERMANY
Tel: +49 (0) 2203 1021910
Fax: +49 (0) 2203 1023551
Email: info@designeryarns.de

SWEDEN
Hamilton Yarns
Storgatan 14
64730 Mariefred
Tel/Fax: +46 (0) 1591 2006
www.hamiltondesign.biz

FINLAND
Eiran Tukku
Makelankatu 54B
00510 Helsinki
Tel: +358 503460575
Email: maria.hellbom@eirantukku.fi

NORWAY
Viking of Norway
Bygdaveien 63
4333 Oltedal
Tel: +47 51611660
Fax: +47 51616235
Email: post@viking-garn.no
www.viking-garn.no

FRANCE
Plassard Diffusion
La Filature
71800 Varennes-sous-Dun
Tel: +33 (0) 385282828
Fax: +33 (0) 385282829
Email: info@laines-plassard.com

AUSTRALIA/NEW ZEALAND
Prestige Yarns Pty Ltd.
P.O. Box 39
Bulli, New South Wales 2516
AUSTRALIA
Tel: +61 24 285 6669
Email: info@prestigeyarns.com
www.prestigeyarns.com

SPAIN
Oyambre Needlework
SL Balmes, 200 At. 4
08006 Barcelona
Tel: +34 (0) 93 487 26 72
Fax: +34 (0) 93 218 6694
Email: info@oyambreonline.com

JAPAN
Eisaku Noro & Co Ltd.
55 Shimoda Ohibino Azaichou
Ichinomiya, Aichi 491 0105
Tel: +81 586 51 3113
Fax: +81 586 51 2625
Email: noro@io.ocn.ne.jp
www.eisakunoro.com

RUSSIA
Fashion Needlework
Evgenia Rodina, Ul. Nalichnaya, 27
St. Petersburg 199226
Tel: +7 (812) 928-17-39,
(812) 350-56-76, (911) 988-60-03
Email: knitting.info@gmail.com
www.fashion-rukodelie.ru

Index